Grit in the Oyster

Grit in the Oyster

Inspirational quotes from the creative world

UNICORN

I can't think of anyone I admire
who isn't fuelled by self-doubt.
It's an essential ingredient.
It's the grit in the oyster.

Sir Richard Eyre

English film, theatre, television and opera director.

I DON'T PAINT OUT
OF RESPONSIBILITY.
I PAINT OUT OF NEED.

Jim Dine

urge

I was on automatic pilot; ideas for gadgets kept coming, fed by a force of energy flowing through me and around me. I wasn't really conscious of pausing to eat or sleep, I was caught up in a flurry of activity. I must have been experiencing the same sort of rapture of creation I imagine composers or poets get carried away by when they lose themselves in their work. I forgot about everything else to concentrate on what I was doing. I'd work eighteen-hour stretches and fall asleep in my clothes. Then I'd wake up in the middle of the night, brew a pot of tea, and start work again. I was tired, but work had become pure enjoyment.

Trevor Baylis

The creative urge is the demon that will not accept anything second rate.

Agnes de Mille

Without passion man is a mere latent force and possibility, like the flint which awaits the shock of the iron before it can give forth its spark.

Henri-Frédéric Amiel

I have no special talents. I am only passionately curious.

Albert Einstein

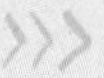

Art is the desire of a man to express himself, to record the reactions of his personality to the world he lives in.

Phil Cousineau

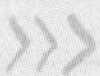

You must love your work as you love a mistress whom you want to glorify. Once you are possessed by the creative urge there is no room for any other drive or thought.

Carl Hauptman

ONE WOULD NEVER UNDERTAKE SUCH A THING IF ONE WERE NOT DRIVEN ON BY SOME DEMON WHOM ONE CAN NEITHER RESIST NOR UNDERSTAND.

George Orwell

TRUE ART IS CHARACTERISED BY AN IRRESISTIBLE URGE IN THE CREATIVE ARTIST.

Albert Einstein

WHEN THE CREATIVE IMPULSE SWEEPS OVER YOU, GRAB IT. YOU GRAB IT AND HONOUR IT AND USE IT, BECAUSE MOMENTUM IS A RARE GIFT.

Justina Chen

Art has always been a big part of my DNA. As a child I would lose myself for hours and hours painting, which I later realised was also a way of expressing my thoughts and emotions.

Philipp-Rudolph Humm

I almost never start with an image. I start with a painting idea, an impulse, usually derived from my own world.

Robert Motherwell

I go to the studio every day because one day I may go and the Angel will be there. What if I don't go and the Angel comes?

Philip Guston

The painter's obsession with his subject is all that he needs to drive him to work.

Lucian Freud

I think there is a period of aesthetic discovery that happens to a man and he can do all sorts of things at white heat.

Walker Evans

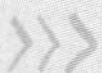

We are image-makers and image-ridden.... We work until we vanish.

Philip Guston

I started producing work with an ecstatic addiction.

Ben Nicholson

WITHOUT PASSION MAN IS A MERE LATENT FORCE AND POSSIBILITY, LIKE THE FLINT WHICH AWAITS THE SHOCK OF THE IRON BEFORE IT CAN GIVE FORTH ITS SPARK.

Henri-Frédéric Amiel

THERE IS A VITALITY,
A LIFE FORCE, AN
ENERGY, A QUICKENING
THAT IS TRANSLATED
THROUGH YOU INTO ACTION,
AND BECAUSE THERE IS
ONLY ONE OF YOU IN ALL
TIME, THIS EXPRESSION
IS UNIQUE. AND IF YOU
BLOCK IT, IT WILL NEVER
EXIST THROUGH ANY
OTHER MEDIUM AND
WILL BE LOST.

Martha Graham

THE URGE FOR DESTRUCTION IS ALSO A CREATIVE URGE!

Mikhail Bakunin

PASSION, THOUGH A BAD REGULATOR, IS A POWERFUL SPRING.

Ralph Waldo Emerson

I must create a system or be
enslaved by another man's. I
will not reason and compare;
my business is to create.
William Blake

Man is a creative animal,
doomed to strive towards
a goal, engaged in
full-time engineering.
Fyodor Dostoevsky

Art is when you hear a
knocking from your soul –
and you answer.
Terri Guillemets

You ask me why I spend
my life writing? Do I find
entertainment? Is it
worthwhile? Above all, does
it pay? If not, then, is there
a reason?... I write only
because there is a voice
within me. That will
not be still.
Sylvia Plath

The truly creative mind in
any field is no more than this:
A human creature born
abnormally, inhumanly
sensitive. To him ... a touch
is a blow, a sound is a noise,
a misfortune is a tragedy,
a joy is an ecstasy, a friend
is a lover, a lover is a god,
and failure is death. Add to
this cruelly delicate organism
the overpowering necessity to
create, create, create – so that
without the creating of music
or poetry or books or buildings
or something of meaning, his
very breath is cut off from him.
He must create, must pour
out creation. By some strange,
unknown, inward urgency
he is not really alive unless
he is creating.
Pearl S. Buck

Write while the heat is in you.
The writer who postpones
the recording of his thoughts
uses an iron which has cooled
to burn a hole with. He
cannot inflame the minds
of his audience.
Henry David Thoreau

YOU MUST LOVE YOUR
WORK AS YOU LOVE
A MISTRESS WHOM
YOU WANT TO GLORIFY.
ONCE YOU ARE
POSSESSED BY THE
CREATIVE URGE THERE
IS NO ROOM FOR ANY
OTHER DRIVE OR
THOUGHT.

Carl Hauptman

THE STATE OF MIND
WHICH ENABLES A MAN
TO DO WORK OF THIS KIND
IS AKIN TO THAT OF THE
RELIGIOUS WORSHIPER
OR THE LOVER; THE
DAILY EFFORT COMES
FROM NO DELIBERATE
INTENTION OR PROGRAMME,
BUT STRAIGHT FROM
THE HEART.

Albert Einstein

ONE CAN NEVER CONSENT TO CRAWL WHEN ONE FEELS AN IMPULSE TO SOAR.

Helen Keller

I WANT TO PUT A DING IN THE UNIVERSE.

Steve Jobs

PERSONALLY, I BELIEVE VERY MUCH IN VALUES OF SAVAGERY; I MEAN: INSTINCT, PASSION, MOOD, VIOLENCE, MADNESS.

Henri-Frédéric Amiel

ART IS THE MOST FRENZIED ORGY MAN IS CAPABLE OF.

Jean Dubuffet

PHOTOGRAPHY MY PASSION, THE SEARCH FOR TRUTH, MY OBSESSION.

Alfred Stieglitz

I MEAN, ART FOR ART'S SAKE IS RIDICULOUS. ART IS FOR THE SAKE OF ONE'S NEEDS.

Carl Andre

PART OF UNDERSTANDING THE CREATIVE URGE IS UNDERSTANDING THAT IT'S PRIMAL. WANTING TO CHANGE THE WORLD IS NOT A NOBLE CALLING, IT'S A PRIMAL CALLING.

Hugh Macleod

WHEN I CAN NO LONGER CREATE ANYTHING, I'LL BE DONE FOR.

Coco Chanel

I KNOW JUST HOW FRUSTRATING IT CAN BE WHEN YOU'RE TIRED AND EXHAUSTED, BUT YOU STILL WANT TO DRAW SOMETHING.

Ward Jenkins

FEELING AND LONGING ARE THE MOTIVE FORCES BEHIND ALL HUMAN ENDEAVOUR AND HUMAN CREATIONS.

Albert Einstein

I WILL BE AN ARTIST OR NOTHING!

Eugene O'Neill

ART IS A FRUIT THAT GROWS IN MAN, LIKE A FRUIT ON A PLANT, OR A CHILD IN ITS MOTHER'S WOMB.

Hans Jean Arp

PASSION IS THE FORCE THAT SPRINGS AN ARTIST FROM THE NEEDLING CUSHION OF DEPRESSION.

Robert Glenn

MILLIONS OF MEN
HAVE LIVED TO FIGHT,
BUILD PALACES AND
BOUNDARIES, SHAPE
DESTINIES AND
SOCIETIES; BUT THE
COMPELLING FORCE OF
ALL TIMES HAS BEEN THE
FORCE OF ORIGINALITY
AND CREATION PROFOUNDLY
AFFECTING THE ROOTS
OF HUMAN SPIRIT.

Ansel Adams

I MERELY DRAW WHAT I SEE.
I DRAW WHAT I FEEL IN MY BODY.

Barbara Hepworth

MY LIFE IS SHAPED BY THE
URGENT NEED TO WANDER
AND OBSERVE, AND MY CAMERA
IS MY PASSPORT.

Steve McCurry

MY ART SPRINGS

FROM MY DESIRE

TO HAVE THINGS IN

THE WORLD WHICH

WOULD OTHERWISE

NEVER BE THERE.

Carl Andre

I just absolutely needed the theatre so desperately – it was my fate; it was where I was running towards. It was the place where I found peace and survival and all kinds of things.

Mark Rylance

Not that painting would have been a release. The reason for doing it is the desire to create. I've got to do it! I've seen that, I can still remember it, I've got to paint it.

Otto Dix

Reality is fabricated out of desire.

Man Ray

The desire to create is one of the deepest yearnings of the human soul.

Deiter F. Uchtdorf

Art is basically made by dissatisfied people who are willing to find some means to relieve the dissatisfaction.

John Chamberlain

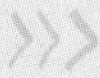

Painting, like passion, is a living voice.

Barnett Newman

I arrived on earth in 1928. Born into a milieu of painters, I acquired my taste for painting with my mother's milk.

Yves Klein

The creative habit is like a drug.

Henry Moore

Creation is a drug I can't do without.

Cecil B. de Mille

IDEAS WON'T KEEP. SOMETHING MUST BE DONE ABOUT THEM. WHEN THE IDEA IS NEW ITS CUSTODIANS HAVE FERVOUR, LIVE FOR IT, AND, IF NEED BE, DIE FOR IT.

Alfred North Whitehead

WRITE IT. SHOOT IT.
PUBLISH IT. CROCHET IT,
SAUTÉ IT, WHATEVER – MAKE.

Joss Whedon

PASSION IS ONE GREAT FORCE
THAT UNLEASHES CREATIVITY,
BECAUSE IF YOU'RE PASSIONATE
ABOUT SOMETHING, YOU'RE
MORE LIKELY TO TAKE RISKS.

Yo-Yo Ma

I PAINT MY OWN REALITY. THE ONLY THING I KNOW IS THAT I PAINT BECAUSE I NEED TO, AND I PAINT WHATEVER PASSES THROUGH MY HEAD WITHOUT ANY OTHER CONSIDERATION.

Frida Kahlo

YOU CAN'T WAIT FOR INSPIRATION, YOU HAVE TO GO AFTER IT WITH A CLUB.

Jack London

IDEAS ARE LIKE RABBITS. YOU GET A COUPLE AND LEARN HOW TO HANDLE THEM, AND PRETTY SOON YOU HAVE A DOZEN.

John Steinbeck

AN INVASION OF ARMIES CAN BE RESISTED, BUT NOT AN IDEA WHOSE TIME HAS COME.

Victor Hugo

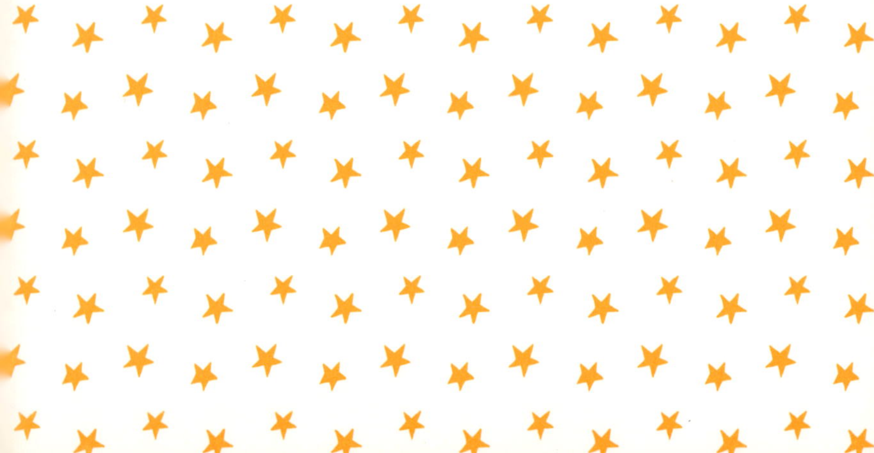

I'm not that obsessed with making representations of ugliness. Everything I've seen is beautiful....

Otto Dix

In the war (at the machine factory at Wülfen) I discovered my love for the wheel and realised that machines are abstractions of the human spirit.

Kurt Schwitters

For a number of years Jazz had a tremendous influence on my thoughts about art and life.

Stuart Davis

I have taught my students not to apply rules or mechanical ways of seeing.

Joseph Albers

I believe that nothing can be more abstract, more unreal, than what we actually see. We know that ... the objective world ... never really exists as we see and understand it ... has no intrinsic meaning of its own, such as the meanings that we attach to it.

Giorgio Morandi

Seeing the life around, clearly and vividly, is something that is exciting in its own right, is an innate gift, varying in intensity with the individual's temperament and environment.

Bill Brandt

In our life there is a single colour, as on an artist's palette, which provides the meaning of life and art. It is the colour of love.

Marc Chagall

I paint not the things I see but the feelings they arouse in me.
Franz Kline

Creativity is that marvellous capacity to grasp mutually distinct realities and draw a spark from their juxtaposition.
Max Ernst

All important things in art have always originated from the deepest feeling about the mystery of Being.
Max Beckmann

Inspiration is a farce that poets have invented to give themselves importance.
Jean Anouilh

Art is viable when it finds elements in the surrounding environment. Our ancestors drew their subject matter from the religious attitudes which weighed on their souls. We must now learn to draw inspiration from the tangible miracles around us.
Umberto Boccioni

Colours in vibration, peeling like silver bells and clanging like bronze bells, proclaiming happiness, passion and love, soul, blood and death.
Emil Nolde

Fill your paper with the breathings of your heart.
William Wordsworth

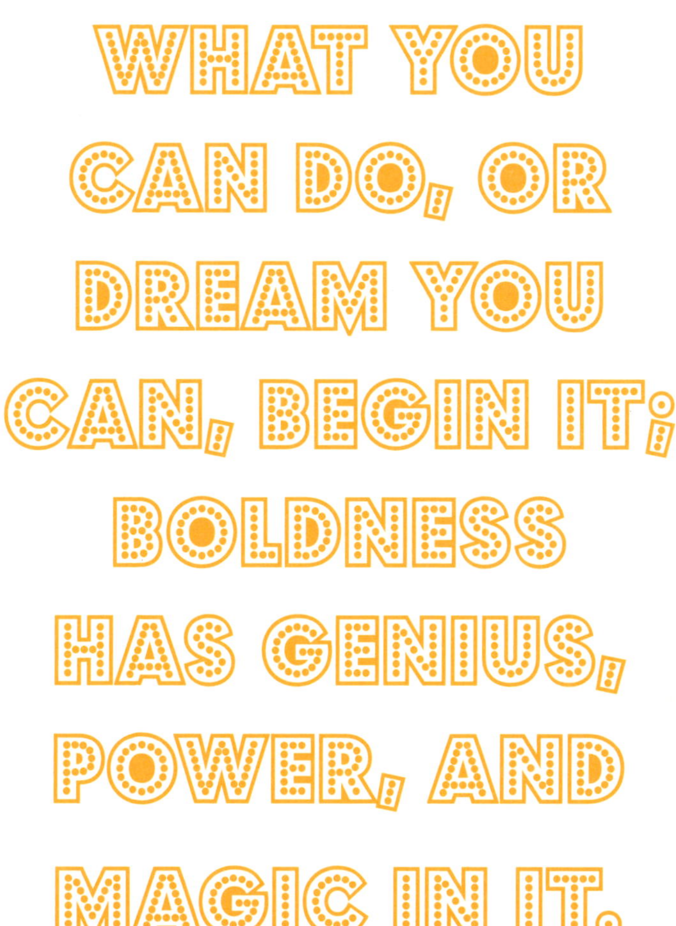

Johann Wolfgang von Goethe

IF YOU BELIEVE IN AN IDEA,
YOU DON'T OWN IT,
IT OWNS YOU.

Raymond Chandler

I PAINT SELF-PORTRAITS
BECAUSE I AM SO OFTEN ALONE,
BECAUSE I AM THE PERSON I
KNOW BEST. I AM MY OWN MUSE.
THE SUBJECT I KNOW THE BEST.

Frida Kahlo

DO NOT FEAR TO BE ECCENTRIC IN OPINION, FOR EVERY OPINION NOW ACCEPTED WAS ONCE ECCENTRIC.

Bertrand Russell

That was the Alka-Seltzer moment, the moment when the tablet hits the water and begins to fizz.

Trevor Baylis

It isn't that inspiration doesn't exist, but it comes only with writing.

John Braine

I have found that sitting in a place where you have never sat before can be inspiring.

Dodie Smith

One can be instructed in society; one is inspired only in solitude.

Johann Wolfgang von Goethe

Better beware of notions like genius and inspiration; they are a sort of magic wand and should be used sparingly by anybody who wants to see things clearly.

José Ortega y Gasset

And Archimedes, as he was washing, thought of a manner of computing the proportion of gold in King Hiero's crown by seeing the water flowing over the bathing-stool. He leaped up as one possessed or inspired, crying, 'I have found it! Eureka!'.

Plutarch

I dream my painting and I paint my dream.

Vincent Van Gogh

I USE THE GALLERY AS IF IT WERE A DOCTOR. I COME FOR IDEAS AND HELP – TO LOOK AT SITUATIONS WITHIN PAINTING, RATHER THAN PAINTINGS.

Lucian Freud

AN ARTIST PAINTS, DANCES, DRAWS, WRITES, DESIGNS, OR ACTS AT THE EXPANDING EDGE OF CONSCIOUSNESS. WE PRESS INTO THE UNKNOWN RATHER THAN THE KNOWN. THIS MAKES LIFE LOVELY AND LIVELY.

Julia Cameron

GO AND MAKE INTERESTING MISTAKES, MAKE AMAZING MISTAKES, MAKE GLORIOUS AND FANTASTIC MISTAKES. BREAK RULES. LEAVE THE WORLD MORE INTERESTING FOR YOUR BEING HERE. MAKE. GOOD. ART.

Neil Gaiman

A man would do well to carry a pencil in his pocket and write down the thoughts of the moment. Those that come unsought for are commonly the most valuable and should be secured because they seldom return.

Francis Bacon

The 'germ,' wherever gathered, has ever been for me, 'the germ of a story', and most of the stories strained to shape under my hand have sprung from a single small seed, a seed as remote and windblown as a casual hint.

Henry James

The problem is never how to get new, innovative thoughts into your mind, but how to get old ones out ... Clean out a corner of your mind and creativity will instantly fill it.

Dee Hock

When I am travelling in a carriage, or walking after a good meal, or during the night when I cannot sleep; it is on such occasions that ideas flow best and most abundantly.

Wolfgang Amadeus Mozart

All the really good ideas I ever had came to me while I was milking a cow.

Grant Wood

The one thing that you have that nobody else has is you. Your voice, your mind, your story, your vision. So write and draw and build and play and dance and live as only you can.

Neil Gaiman

Dance first, think later.

Samuel Beckett

TO SEE A WORLD IN A GRAIN OF SAND, AND HEAVEN IN A WILD FLOWER; TO HOLD INFINITY IN THE PALM OF YOUR HAND AND ETERNITY IN AN HOUR – IS INSPIRATION.

William Blake

PART OF WHAT I'M ABOUT IS SEEING HOW I CAN PAINT THE SAME THING DIFFERENTLY INSTEAD OF DIFFERENT THINGS THE SAME WAY.

Alex Katz

GRAFFITI IS ONE OF THE FEW TOOLS YOU HAVE IF YOU HAVE ALMOST NOTHING. AND EVEN IF YOU DON'T COME UP WITH A PICTURE TO CURE WORLD POVERTY YOU CAN MAKE SOMEONE SMILE WHILE THEY'RE HAVING A PISS.

Banksy

JUST DON'T GIVE UP TRYING TO DO WHAT YOU REALLY WANT TO DO. WHERE THERE'S LOVE AND INSPIRATION, I DON'T THINK YOU CAN GO WRONG.

Ella Fitzgerald

We shape clay into a pot. But it is the emptiness inside that holds whatever we want.

Tao saying

I don't believe in total freedom for the artist. Left on his own, free to do anything he likes, the artist ends up doing nothing at all. If there's one thing that's dangerous for an artist, it's precisely this question of total freedom, waiting for inspiration and all the rest of it.

Federico Fellini

The problem is never how to get new, innovative thoughts into your mind, but how to get old ones out. Every mind is a building filled with archaic furniture. Clean out a corner of your mind and creativity will instantly fill it.

Dee Hock

Those who do not want to imitate anything, produce nothing.

Salvador Dalí

In art, the hand can never execute anything higher than the heart can imagine.

Ralph Waldo Emerson

What moves men of genius, or rather what inspires their work, is not new ideas, but their obsession with the idea that what has already been said is still not enough.

Eugène Delacroix

Writing is like walking in a deserted street. Out of the dust in the street you make a mud pie.

John le Carré

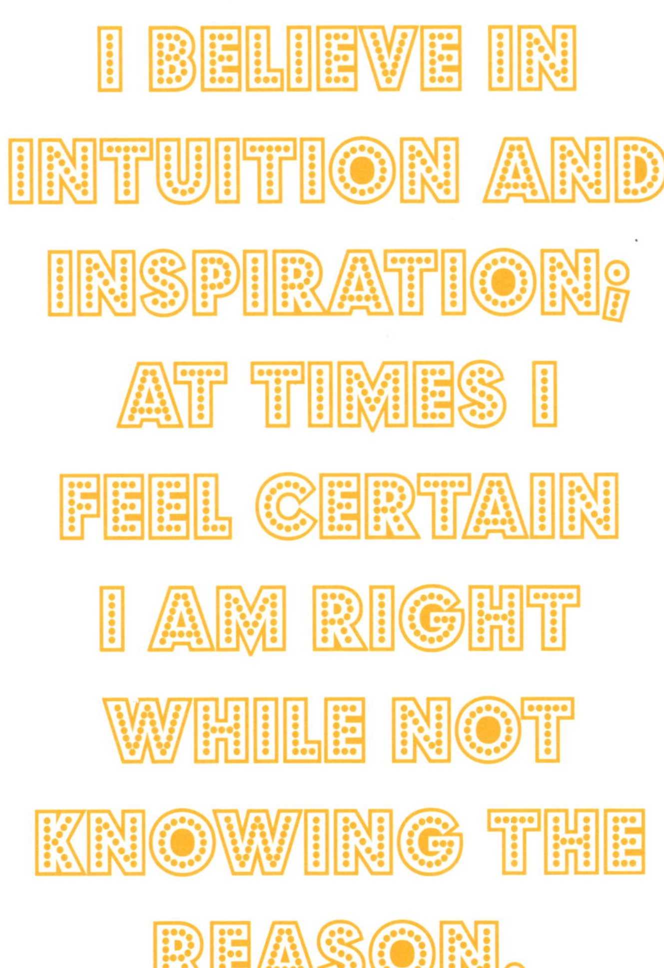

Albert Einstein

INSPIRATION IS THERE ALL THE TIME. FOR EVERYONE WHOSE MIND IS NOT CLOUDED OVER WITH THOUGHTS WHETHER THEY REALISE IT OR NOT.

Agnes Martin

I'LL ALWAYS BE GRATEFUL TO RENT COLLECTING. I'VE PUT MANY OF THE TENANTS IN MY PICTURES.

L.S. Lowry

ALL GREAT DEEDS AND ALL GREAT THOUGHTS HAVE A RIDICULOUS BEGINNING.

Albert Camus

MY WISH IS THAT WE MIGHT PROGRESSIVELY LOSE OUR CONFIDENCE IN WHAT WE THINK WE BELIEVE AND THE THINGS WE CONSIDER STABLE AND SECURE, IN ORDER TO REMIND OURSELVES OF THE INFINITE NUMBER OF THINGS STILL WAITING TO BE DISCOVERED.

Antoni Tàpies

CREATIVITY IS MISTAKES.

Grayson Perry

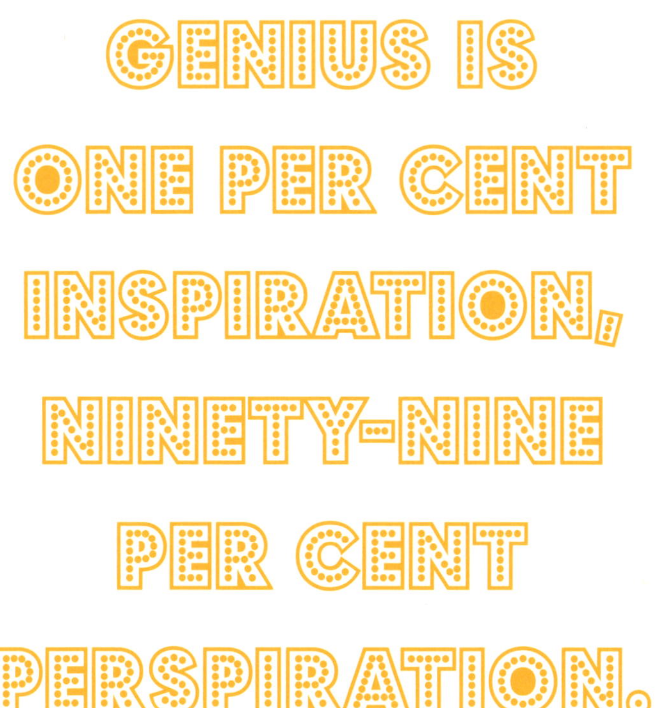

Thomas Edison

SCULPTURE IS LIKE ARCHAEOLOGY: YOU DIG IN AND YOU FIND SOMETHING.

Georg Baselitz

THE GREAT SCIENTIST DARES TO DIFFER FROM ACCEPTED 'FACTS' – THINK IRRATIONALLY – LET THE ARTIST DO LIKEWISE.

Edward Weston

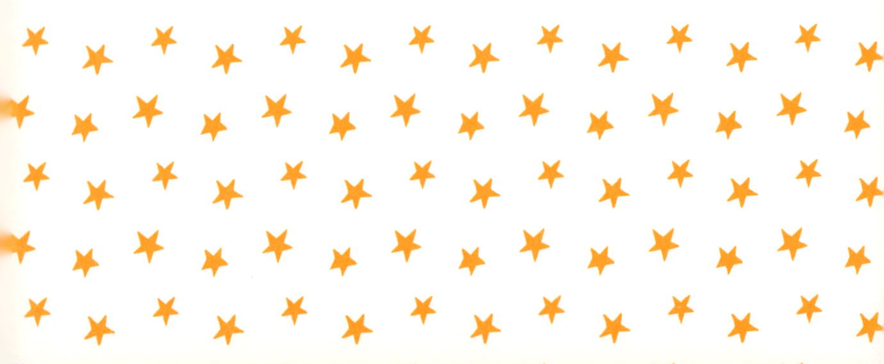

Write while the heat is in you. The writer who postpones the recording of his thoughts uses an iron which has cooled to burn a hole with. He cannot inflame the minds of his audience.
Henry David Thoreau

Inspiration is wonderful when it happens, but the writer must develop an approach for the rest of the time.... The wait is simply too long.
Leonard Bernstein

I throw a spear into the darkness. That is intuition. Then I must send an army into the darkness to find the spear. That is intellect.
Ingmar Bergam

Discovery consists of looking at the same thing as everyone else and thinking something different.
Albert Szent-Györgyi

When the creative impulse sweeps over you, grab it. You grab it and honour it and use it, because momentum is a rare gift.
Justina Chen

I think if you have any connections with the arts you have got to be interested in music and poetry and sculpture and painting – the whole lot. Because I feel that artists are influenced within themselves, within their friends and within writers and artists of the past.
Gordon Beningfield

PAINT THE FLYING SPIRIT OF THE BIRD RATHER THAN ITS FEATHERS.

Robert Henri

DO SOMETHING WONDERFUL, PEOPLE MAY IMITATE IT.

Albert Schweitzer

SOME PEOPLE FEEL THE RAIN. OTHERS JUST GET WET.

Bob Marley

INSPIRATION IS A GUEST THAT DOES NOT WILLINGLY VISIT THE LAZY.

Pyotr Tchaikovsky

ONE LEARNS ABOUT
PAINTING BY LOOKING
AT AND IMITATING
OTHER PAINTERS.

Frank Stella

I TRY TO APPLY COLOURS
LIKE WORDS THAT SHAPE
POEMS, LIKE NOTES THAT
SHAPE MUSIC.

Joan MirÓ

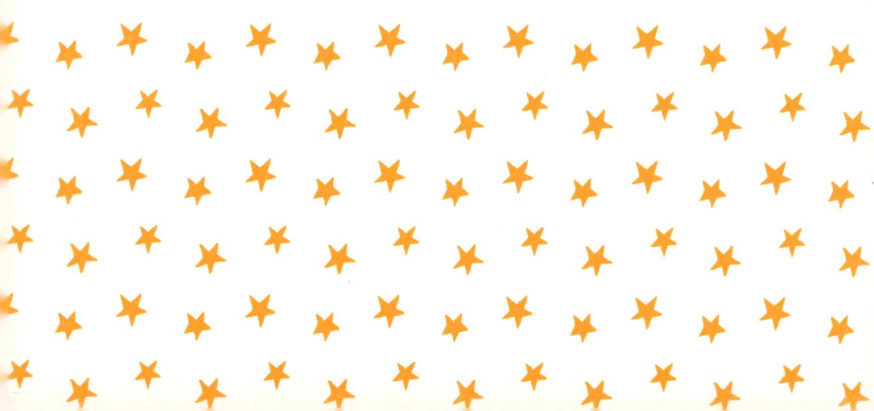

Great art picks up
where nature ends.
Marc Chagall

Don't bend; water it down;
or make it logical; don't
edit your soul for fashion.
Follow intense obsessions
mercilessly.
Franz Kafka

Great things are not
accomplished by those
who yield to trends and fads
and popular opinion.
Jack Kerouac

To practise any art, no
matter how well or badly,
is a way to make your
soul grow. So do it.
Kurt Vonnegut

Be silent, or say something
better than silence.
Pythagoras

The world is full of
magic things, patiently
waiting for our senses
to grow sharper.
William B. Yeats

There are not more than
five musical notes, yet the
combinations of these five give
rise to more melodies than
can ever be heard. There are
not more than five primary
colours, yet in combination
they produce more hues than
can ever be seen. There
are not more than five
cardinal tastes, yet
combinations of them yield
more flavours than can
ever be tasted.
Sun Tzu, *The Art of War*

Sometimes you gotta create
what you want to be part of.
Geri Weitzman

Give what you have.
To someone else it may be
better than you dare to think.
Henry Wadsworth Longfellow

I shut my eyes in order to see.
Paul Gauguin

Being an author is having
angels whisper in your ear –
and devils, too.
Graycie Harmon

A rock pile ceases to be a
rock pile the moment a single
man contemplates it, bearing
within him the image of
a cathedral.
Antoine de Saint-Exupéry

As long as you've got
slightly more perception
than the average wrapped
loaf, you are capable of
inventing something.
Trevor Baylis

Straight-away the ideas
flow in upon me, directly
from God, and not only
do I see distinct themes
in my mind's eye, but they
are clothed in the right
forms, harmonies
and orchestration.
Johannes Brahms

In writing songs I've learned
as much from Cézanne as I
have from Woody Guthrie.
Bob Dylan

Creativity is intelligence
having fun.
Albert Einstein

DON'T TRUST A BRILLIANT IDEA UNLESS IT SURVIVES THE HANGOVER.

Jimmy Breslin

THE ARTIST IS A RECEPTACLE
FOR EMOTIONS THAT COME
FROM ALL OVER THE PLACE:
FROM THE SKY, FROM THE EARTH,
FROM A SCRAP OF PAPER,
FROM A PASSING SHAPE,
FROM A SPIDER'S WEB.

Pablo Picasso

I SIT IN THE DARK AND WAIT
FOR A LITTLE FLAME TO
APPEAR AT THE END OF
MY PENCIL.

Billy Collins

THERE ARE PAINTERS WHO TRANSFORM THE SUN TO A YELLOW SPOT, BUT THERE ARE OTHERS WHO, WITH THE HELP OF THEIR ART AND THEIR INTELLIGENCE, TRANSFORM A YELLOW SPOT INTO SUN.

Pablo Picasso

What one does is what counts. Not what one had the intention of doing.

Pablo Picasso

I like to make historical references to the bad things of the past so that the younger generations do not make the same mistakes.

Philipp-Rudolph Humm

The object of art is not to reproduce reality, but to create a reality of the same intensity.

Alberto Giacometti

I think that you've got to make something that pleases you and hope that other people feel the same way.

Thomas Keller

Art must be an expression of love or it is nothing. If I create from the heart, nearly everything works; if from the head, almost nothing.

Marc Chagall

The artist must try to raise the level of taste of the masses, not debase himself to the level of unformed and impoverished taste.

Diego Rivera

I do not belong to any school, I simply want to do something that is personal to my self.

Edouard Vuillard

I remember Francis Bacon would say that he felt he was giving art what he thought it previously lacked. With me, it's what Yeats called the fascination with what's difficult. I'm only trying to do what I can't do.

Lucian Freud

I'm interested only in expressing basic human emotions. And the fact that a lot of people break down and cry when confronted with my pictures shows that I can communicate these basic human emotions.

Mark Rothko

Draw the art you want to see, start the business you want to run, play the music you want to hear, write the books you want to read, build the products you want to use – do the work you want to see done.

Austin Kleon

I want to show an audience that it's okay to feel out of place in a mad world; that if they feel depressed or frightened or lonely when confronted with the deranged excesses of contemporary society then they're not dysfunctional – they're right to feel that way.

Guy Denning

The whole concept of the free art thing was challenging the notion of art as a commodity and its worth in society. Now I'm taking that to another level, testing the viability of separating art from commerce.

Adam Neate

The principles of true art is not to portray, but to evoke.

Jerry Kosinski

I am not interested in rules and conventions ... photography is not a sport. If I think a picture will look better brilliantly lit, I use lights, or even flash. It is the result that counts, no matter how it was achieved.

Bill Brandt

Intent is not a thought, or an object, or a wish. Intent is what can make a man succeed when his thoughts tell him that he is defeated.

Carlos Castaneda

Working on these paintings, there's always an idea which is an ideal. It's always impossible.... But I think every time, maybe, I just get closer to some impossible thing....

Brice Marden

Our primary function is to create an emotion and our secondary function is to sustain that emotion.

Alfred Hitchcock

To feel the soul without explaining it, without vocabulary, and to represent this sensation.

Yves Klein

I'm interested in locating the holy grail of the minimum means to express the most complex ideas.

Ben Nicolson

Art should startle the viewer into thinking about the meaning of life.

Antoni Tapies

I can't resist having a joke. Artists I like, such as Breugel, put jokes in their work. I think it's part of reflecting human life.

Grayson Perry

If I didn't think what I was doing had something to do with enlarging the boundaries of art, I wouldn't go on doing it.

Claes Oldenburg

Are we to paint what's on the face, what's inside the face, or what's behind it?

Pablo Picasso

Unlike the expressionists, I have never been interested in renewing the world through the vehicle of art.

Georg Baselitz

The still must tease with the promise of a story the viewer of it itches to be told.

Cindy Sherman

For that is the power of the camera: seize the familiar and give it new meanings, a special significance by the mark of a personality.

Alfred Stieglitz

The force of art lies in its immediate influence on human psychology and in its active contagiousness.

Naum Gabo

Maybe this is a utopian view of art but I do believe that art can function as a vehicle, that it isn't just a cultural pursuit, something that happens in art galleries. Unless art is linked to experience and the fear and joy of that, it becomes mere icing on the cake.

Anthony Gormley

Dare to dream! If you did not have the capability to make your wildest wishes come true, your mind would not have the capacity to conjure such ideas in the first place. There is no limitation on what you can potentially achieve, except for the limitation you choose to impose on your own imagination. What you believe to be possible will always come to pass – to the extent that you deem it possible. It really is as simple as that.

Anthon St.Maarten

Every journey begins with the first step of articulating the intention, and then becoming the intention.

Bryant McGill

Sculpture is an art of the open air.... I would rather have a piece of my sculpture put in a landscape, almost any landscape, than in, or on, the most beautiful building I know.

Henry Moore

Any art worthy of its name should address life, man, nature, death and tragedy.

Barnet Newmann

Intention and awareness are the two tools that enable us to create anything our heart desires from the universe.

Russell Eric Dobda

I am interested
in art as a means
of living a life;
not as a means of
making a living.

Jimmy Breslin

I'm not really sure what social message my art carries, if any. And I don't really want it to carry one.

Roy Lichtenstein

The value of art lies in its power to increase our moral force or establish its heightening influence.

Odilon Redon

I think art is about human existence. Almost by default I'm expressing my experiences as a human.

Robert Gober

Intention is one of the most powerful forces there is. What you mean when you do a thing will always determine the outcome. The law creates the world.

Brenna Yovanoff

The main thing
is to be moved,
to love, to hope,
to tremble,
to live.

Auguste Rodin

I would like to show the world today as an ant sees it, and tomorrow as the moon sees it.

Hannah Hoch

The life of every man is a diary in which he means to write one story, and writes another.

J.M. Barrie

Powerful words come with powerful intent. Where you have passion, strength, courage, and determination you can accomplish anything!

K.L. Toth

The act of speaking our intentions aloud shifts them from wishful thinking into action.

Michael Thomas Sunnarborg

To change any behaviour we have to slow down and act intentionally rather than from habit and impulse.

Henna Inam

It is more important to be of pure intention than of perfect action.

Ilyas Kassam

At some point
everyone must
decide if they are
a creator or a critic,
a lover or a hater,
a giver or a taker.

Anon

The intention (of an artist) is (the same as a scientist) ... to discover and reveal what is unsuspected but significant in life.

H.W. Leggett

You don't make art out of good intentions.

Gustave Flaubert

To become great, you must choose to allocate your time to your greatest opportunities. You will have to choose to spend time on the difficult things that create your biggest payoffs. To be great you will need to live with intention. That will require you to be clear on what matters most, and then to have the courage to say no to things that distract you.

Brian P. Moran

There comes a time when all we dream, all we do, all we are combines in an abstract way with all we can be. These notions, however vague, intertwine with others and acts like a balm, an easy awakening of some forgotten sense. We are after all the sum of our intentions.

Becca Horne

Perfection does not mean errorless. Real perfection starts with real intention and ends with delivery, all driven by seeking knowledge, trial and error and investing emotions. Whatever's delivered after that is perfect.

Sameh Elsayed

Art is meant to disturb, science reassures.

Georges Braque

The sound of the sea, the curve of a horizon, wind in leaves, the cry of a bird leave manifold impressions in us. And suddenly, without our wishing it at all, one of these memories spills from us and finds expression in musical language.... I want to sing my interior landscape with the simple artlessness of a child.

Claude Debussy

I feel that when I am painting, it is a form of worship. I see how wonderful nature is and how wonderful art is ... and by trying to produce these works of art, I feel that I am just showing my appreciation of these creations.

E. J. Hughes

When I photograph, what I'm really doing is seeking answers to things.

Wynn Bullock

The state of mind which enables a man to do work of this kind is akin to that of the religious worshiper or the lover; the daily effort comes from no deliberate intention or program, but straight from the heart.

Albert Einstein

The aim of every artist is to arrest motion, which is life, by artificial means and hold it fixed so that a hundred years later, when a stranger looks at it, it moves again since it is life.

William Faulkner

Painting is an attempt to come to terms with life. There are as many solutions as there are human beings.

George Tooker

Don't try to figure out what other people want to hear from you; figure out what you have to say. It's the one and only thing you have to offer.

Barbara Kingsolver

I can never accomplish what I want – only what I would have wanted had I thought of it beforehand.

Richard Diebenkorn

Everything you do doesn't need praise. If you're aware of your intention the glory is already yours.

Alexandra Elle

The object isn't to make art, it's to be in that wonderful state which makes art inevitable.

Robert Henri

Quality is never an accident,
it is always the result of an
intelligent effort.
John Ruskin

It is my duty to voice
the sufffering of men, the
never-ending sufferings
heaped mountain high.
Kathe Kollwitz

Typographical design should
perform optically what the
speaker creates through voice
and gesture of his thoughts.
El Lissitzky

The purpose of art is to raise
people to a higher level of
awareness than they would
otherwise attain on their own.
Brassai

One doesn't need to know
the artist's private intentions.
The work tells all.
Susan Sontag

I am engaged with ideas
of humanism, existential
questions of life, consumerism
and the impact of technology
upon the human condition.
Philipp-Rudolf Humm

I never have taken a
picture I've intended.
They're always
better or worse.
Diane Arbus

Abstract art should be
enjoyed just as music is
enjoyed – after a while you
may like it or you may not.
Jackson Pollock

I write to give myself strength. I write to be the characters that I am not. I write to explore all the things I'm afraid of.

Joss Whedon

Being the richest
man in the cemetery
doesn't matter to me.
Going to bed at night
saying we've done
something wonderful
... that's what
matters to me.

Steve Jobs

I would rather be ashes than dust! I would rather that my spark should burn out in a brilliant blaze than it should be stifled by dry-rot. I would rather be a superb meteor, every atom of me in magnificent glow, than a sleepy and permanent planet. The function of man is to live, not to exist. I shall not waste my days trying to prolong them. I shall use my time.

Jack London

The artist never entirely knows – we guess. We may be wrong, but we take leap after leap in the dark.

Agnes de Mille

When it is working, you completely go into another place, you're tapping into things that are totally universal, completely beyond your ego and your own self. That's what it's all about.

Keith Haring

Do not go where the path
may lead, go instead
where there is no path
and leave a trail.
Ralph Waldo Emerson

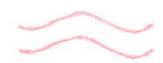

To find one's way anywhere
one has to find one's door, just
like Alice, you see. You take
too much of one thing and
you get too big, then you
take too much of another
and you get too small.
You've got to find your own
doorway into things....
Paula Rego

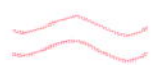

It may be that when we
no longer know what to do,
we have come to our real
work, and when we no longer
know which way to go,
we have begun our
real journey.
Wendell Berry

From inaccessible
mountain range by
way of desert untrod
by human foot to the
ends of the unknown
seas, the breath of the
everlasting creative spirit
is felt, rejoicing over
every speck of dust that
hearkens to it and lives.
Johann Wolfgang von Goethe

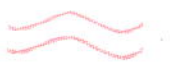

The artist is always
beginning. Any work of art
which is not a beginning,
an invention, a discovery
is of little worth.
Ezra Pound

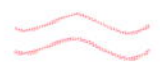

To see far is one thing,
going there is another.
Constantin Brâncusi

I was with a man and he said, look, and there I saw it. It changed my life. From then on I devoted myself to it. I have never tired of looking. It is always fresh.

L.S. Lowry

Being an artist is a very long game. It is not a 10-year game. I hope I'll be around making art when I'm 80.

Anish Kapoor

It takes a lot of time to be a genius. You have to sit around so much doing nothing, really doing nothing.

Gertrude Stein

When I went to New York in 1986, I met a bunch of guys that were subway painters and I saw the work of Jenny Holzer and John Fekner. These people were the godfathers of street art. They had a movement, and I was so impressed by them that it certainly changed the way I was thinking and steered my work into another direction.

Stormie Mills

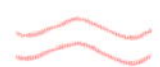

One of the greatest moments of Mother's life came when she found that I, a mere baby, was never so content as with pencil and paper; even before I could speak or walk, I drew. There was no question of my purpose in life.

Dame Laura Knight

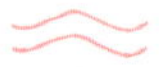

Painting is a very slow art. It doesn't travel with the speed of light. That's why dead painters shine so bright.

Marlene Dumas

The new talent will only emerge from where it has lain hidden if the climate and conditions are propitious.

Michael Cardew

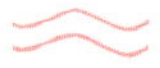

I would like to continue being radical. As you get older, some of the world catches up and it's passed you. In the '60s you were on the crest of a wave because you were part of the wave. I don't want be a stick in the mud and do the same thing as I did last year, I want to do something different and see what happens.

Anthony Caro

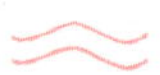

Every generation renews itself in its own way; there's always a reaction against whatever is standard.

Sol LeWitt

We must walk consciously only part way toward our goal, and then leap in the dark to our success.

Henry David Thoreau

One must go through life, be it red or blue, stark naked and accompanied by the music of a subtle fisherman, prepared at all times for a celebration.

Francis Picabia

I always thought of photography as a naughty thing to do – that was one of my favorite things about it, and when I first did it, I felt very perverse.

Diane Arbus

So I made unpleasant sculptures – and now they aren't unpleasant any more. That's the way it goes.

Georg Baselitz

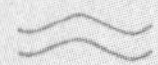

I don't decide in advance that I am going to paint a definite experience, but in the act of painting, it becomes a genuine experience for me.

Franz Kline

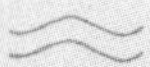

When something is finished, that means it's dead, doesn't it? I believe in everlastingness. I never finish a painting – I just stop working on it for a while.

Arshile Gorky

What an artist learns matters little. What he himself discovers has a real worth for him, and gives him the necessary incitement to work.

Emil Nolde

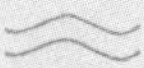

The golden age has not passed; it lies in the future.

Paul Signac

The artist is always engaged in writing a detailed history of the future because he is the only person aware of the nature of the present.

Wyndham Lewis

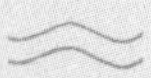

One is also reminded of how, in art, the tortoise so often overtakes the hare...

Clement Greenberg

Do not be afraid to take a big step if one is indicated. You cannot cross a chasm in two small jumps.

David Lloyd George

We have to continually be jumping off cliffs and developing our wings on the way down.

Kurt Vonnegut

If an artist has no experience before he makes a painting or a sculpture, he is not an artist.

Naum Gabo

All that is gold does not glitter; not all those who wander are lost.

J.R.R. Tolkein

A piece of art is never a finished work. It answers a question which has been asked, and asks a new question.

Robert Engman

A moment of complete happiness never occurs in the creation of a work of art. The promise of it is felt in the act of creation but disappears towards the completion of the work. For it is then the painter realises that it is only a picture he is painting. Until then he had almost dared to hope the picture might spring to life.

Lucian Freud

Be brave enough to live life creatively. The creative is the place where no one else has ever been. You have to leave the city of your comfort and go into the wilderness of your intuition. What you'll discover will be wonderful. What you'll discover is yourself.

Alan Alda

To travel hopefully is a better thing than to arrive, and the true success is to labour.

Robert Louis Stevenson

Ideas, like young wine, should be put in storage and taken up again only after they have been allowed to ferment and to ripen.

Richard Strauss

The mind ought to sometimes be diverted that it may return the better to thinking.

Phaedrus

You must not for one instant give up the effort to build new lives for yourselves. Creativity means to push open the heavy, groaning doorway to life. This is not an easy struggle. Indeed, it may be the most difficult task in the world, for opening the door to your own life is, in the end, more difficult than opening the doors to the mysteries of the universe.

Daisaku Ikeda

There is no prescribed route to follow to arrive at a new idea. You have to make the intuitive leap.

Stephen Hawking

The reason that art (writing, engaging, and all of it) is valuable is precisely why I can't tell you how to do it. If there were a map, there'd be no art, because art is the act of navigating without a map.

Seth Godin

Go where the silence is and say something.

Amy Goodman

You cannot discover new oceans unless you have the courage to lose sight of the shore.

André Gide

When in doubt, make a fool of yourself. There is a microscopically thin line between being brilliantly creative and acting like the most gigantic idiot on earth. So what the hell, leap.

Cynthia Heimel

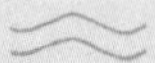

Almost everybody is born a genius and buried an idiot.

Charles Bukowski

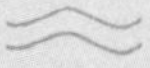

The whole culture is telling you to hurry, while the art tells you to take your time. Always listen to the art.

Junot Diaz

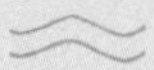

After twenty years you can begin to be sure of what a camera will do.

Brassai

Art reaches its greatest peak when devoid of self-consciousness. Freedom discovers man the moment he loses concern over what impression he is making or about to make.

Bruce Lee

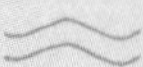

Keep away from people who try to belittle your ambitions. Small people always do that, but the really great ones make you feel that you too can become great.

Mark Twain

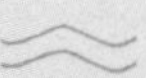

Around here, however, we don't look backwards for very long. We keep moving forward, opening up new doors and doing new things, because we're curious ... and curiosity keeps leading us down new paths.

Walt Disney Company

Nobody can tell you if what you're doing is good, meaningful or worthwhile. The more compelling the path, the more lonely it is.

Hugh Macleod

Artists who seek perfection in everything are those who cannot attain it in anything.

Eugène Delacroix

I do not want to die ... until I have faithfully made the most of my talent and cultivated the seed that was placed in me, until the last small twig has grown.

Käthe Kollwitz

In art, truth and reality begin when one no longer understands what one is doing or what one knows, and when there remains an energy that is all the stronger for being constrained, controlled and compressed.

Henri Matisse

Don't judge each day by the harvest you reap but by the seeds that you plant.

Robert Louis Stevenson

Boredom always precedes a period of great creativity.

Robert M. Pirsig

I had a very happy childhood, but I wasn't that happy a child. I liked being alone and creating characters and voices. I think that's when your creativity is developed, when you're young. I liked the world of the imagination because it was an easy place to go to.

David Walliams

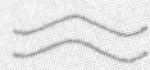

When one door closes, another opens. But we often look so regretfully upon the closed door that we don't see the one which has opened for us.

Alexander Graham Bell

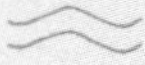

The artist has to be something like a whale swimming with his mouth wide open, absorbing everything until he has what he really needs.

Romare Bearden

Nothing is original. Steal from anywhere that resonates with inspiration or fuels your imagination. Devour old films, new films, music, books, paintings, photographs, poems, dreams, random conversations, architecture, bridges, street signs, trees, clouds, bodies of water, light and shadows. Select only things to steal from that speak directly to your soul. If you do this, your work (and theft) will be authentic. Authenticity is invaluable; originality is non-existent. And don't bother concealing your thievery – celebrate it if you feel like it. In any case, always remember what Jean-Luc Godard said: 'It's not where you take things from – it's where you take them to.'.

Jim Jarmusch

The world is full of fictional characters looking for their stories.

Diane Arbus

[on his deathbed…] Damn, and just when I was starting to get it!

Edgar Degas

Every child is an artist. The problem is how to remain an artist once he grows up.

Pablo Picasso

Remembering that you are going to die is the best way I know to avoid the trap of thinking you have something to lose. You are already naked. There is no reason not to follow your heart.

Steve Jobs

If heaven gives me ten more years (or even an extension of five), I shall certainly become a true artist.

Katsushika Hokusai

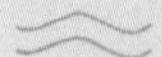

Your time is limited, so don't waste it living someone else's life. Don't be trapped by dogma – which is living with the results of other people's thinking. Don't let the noise of others' opinions drown out your own inner voice. And most important, have the courage to follow your heart and intuition. They somehow already know what you truly want to become. Everything else is secondary.

Steve Jobs

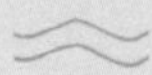

My life and art have not been separated. They have been together.

Eva Hesse

Art is an adventure into an unknown world, which can be explored only by those willing to take risks.

Mark Rothko

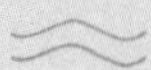

I favour a picture which arrives at its destination without the evidence of a trying journey rather than one which shows the marks of battle.

Charles Sheeler

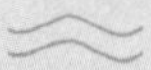

I suffered a nervous breakdown that has lasted a lifetime, though by now I have learned to live with it.

Jeanne Reynal

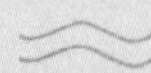

The most important this is to go out and see the stars, not to see them in books.

Edouard Boubat

It is good to have an end to journey towards, but it is the journey that matters in the end.

Ursula Le Guin

Work like you don't need the money. Dance like no one is watching. And love like you've never been hurt.

Mark Twain

Out of clutter, find simplicity. From discord, find harmony. In the middle of difficulty, find opportunity.

Albert Einstein

Art is a magic which makes the hours melt away and even days dissolve into seconds.

Leonora Carrington

My mother said to me, 'If you become a soldier you'll be a general; if you become a monk you'll end up as the Pope.' Instead, I became a painter and wound up as Picasso.

Pablo Picasso

The artist must
create a spark before
he can make a fire,
and before art is born,
the artist must be
ready to be consumed
by the fire of his
own creation.

Auguste Rodin

If you are lucky, and if you live long enough, and if you trust your materials and you trust your instincts, you will see things of beauty growing up in front of you, without you having anything to do with it.

Michael Cardew

I love art so much because of curiosity. At the start of a painting, I know 10 per cent of what the painting will be, and then I have to improvise the whole thing.

Fernando Botero

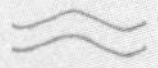

One of the keys to embracing creativity is recognizing that even though it involves risk, you don't die.

David Usher

How often in life we complete a task that was beyond the capability of the person we were when we started it.

Robert Brault

The harder you chase something, the faster you go and the less you're able to let life meet life. If you're having difficulty coming up with new ideas, then slow down.... Creativity exists in the present moment. You can't find it anywhere else.

Natalie Goldberg

There are hundreds of paths up the mountain, all leading to the same place, so it doesn't matter which path you take. The only person wasting time is the one who runs around the mountain, telling everyone that his or her path is wrong.

Hindu proverb

I am seeking. I am striving. I am in it with all my heart.

Vincent van Gogh

A great artist exploits bad moods, set-backs and misfortunes, and converts them into works of art.

Prakash Ghai

When nature wants you to do art, it makes sure that you fail in every venture, other than art. At the end of the day, we can endure much more than we think we can.

Frida Kahlo

Most beginners are too anxious for results. Real progress takes place over a long period of time.

Mary Beth Mackenzie

Everyone has talent at twenty-five. The difficulty is to have it at fifty.

Edgar Degas

When you're an artist you use your own techniques. It's difficult to find a technique and style in art so when you have a style and you see someone else is taking it and reproducing it, you don't like that.

Blek le Rat

It's hard being a girl and a graffiti artist.

Lady Aiko

Most artists are doing basically the same thing – staying off the streets.

Edward Ruscha

The demons are innumerable, arrive at the most inappropriate times, and create panic and terror ... but I have learned that if I can master the negative forces and harness them to my chariot, then they can work to my advantage... Lilies often grow out of carcasses' arseholes.

Ingmar Bergman

For as long as I can remember I have suffered from a deep feeling of anxiety which I have tried to express in my art. Without anxiety and illness I should have been like a ship without a rudder.

Edvard Munch

Our energy is
in proportion to the
resistance it meets.
We attempt nothing great
but from a sense of the
difficulties we have to
encounter, we persevere
in nothing great but
from a pride in
overcoming them.

William Hazlitt

The artist's struggle to transcend his pain can become the seed for many others' hope, transforming a personal journey into a vision for us all.

Diane Cole

My whole life has been nothing more than a continuous struggle against Reaction and the death of art.

Pablo Picasso

I'm very learning-disabled, and I think it drove me to what I'm doing.

Chuck Close

You never paint what you see or think you see. You paint with a thousand vibrations the blow that has struck you: how can you be struck and not cry out in anger?

Nicolas de Stael

I work in waves, because I'm impatient. Because of a certain physicality, of lack of breath from standing. It has to be done and I do take liberties I wouldn't have taken before.

Cy Twombly

My paintings are Battles.

Georg Baselitz

When I do work, I get so much done in such a concentrated time that once I'm through a series, I'm so drained I don't want to get near the camera.

Cindy Sherman

The anarchist painter is not the one who will create anarchist pictures, but the one who will fight with all his individuality against official conventions.

Paul Signac

Contradict yourself. In order to live, you must remain broken up.

Wyndham Lewis

When you look in your mind you find it covered with a lot of rubbishy thoughts. You have to penetrate these and hear what your mind is telling you to do. Such work is original work.

Agnes Martin

For any artist to persevere, they must have an enthusiastic audience of at least one.

Stuart Davis

No one but myself knows the anxiety I go through and the trouble I give myself to finish paintings which do not satisfy me and seem to please so very few others.

Claude Monet

In the end, I feel that one has to have a bit of neurosis to go on being an artist. A balanced human seldom produces art. It's that imbalance which impels us.... The artist lives with anxiety.

Beverley Pepper

Painting what I experience, translating what I feel, is like a great liberation. But it is also work, self-examination, consciousness, criticism, struggle....

Balthus

Art is always to a large extent about need, despair and hopelessness.

Gerhard Richter

I've never met a truly creative person who was happy and satisfied with life.

Terence Conran

In all the creative work that I have done, what has come first is a problem, a puzzle involving discomfort.

Bertrand Russell

Out of suffering have emerged the strongest souls; the most massive characters are seared with scars.

Khalil Gibran

Any idiot can face a crisis; it's this day-to-day living that wears you out.

Anton Chekhov

I've been absolutely terrified every moment of my life and I've never let it keep me from doing a single thing that I wanted to do.

Georgia O'Keefe

My problem painting from my life was I found that you can't paint dirt without romanticising it.

Robert Gober

Every creator painfully experiences the chasm between his inner vision and its ultimate expression.

Isaac Bashevis Singer

I don't have big anxieties. I wish I did. I'd be much more interesting.

Roy Lichtenstein

Adversity is the first path to truth.

Lord George Byron

Accept the challenges so that you may feel the exhilaration of victory.

George S. Patton

The greater the obstacle the more glory in overcoming it.

Jean-Baptiste Moliére

Our greatest weakness lies in giving up. The most certain way to succeed is always to try just one more time.

Thomas A. Edison

There is no success without hardship.

Sophocles

The best work that anybody ever writes is the work that is on the verge of embarrassing him, always.

Arthur Miller

The head is full of books. The hard part is to force them down through the bloodstream and out through the fingers.

Edward Abbey

You should keep on painting no matter how difficult it is, because this is all part of experience, and the more experience you have, the better it is... unless it kills you, and then you know you have gone too far.

Alice Neel

Be daring, be different, be impractical, be anything that will assert integrity of purpose and imaginative vision against the play-it-safers, the creatures of the commonplace, the slaves of the ordinary.

Cecil Beaton

Everyone has talent. What is rare is the courage to follow the talent to the dark place where it leads.

Erica Jong

If it wasn't hard, everyone would do it. It's the hard that makes it great.

Tom Hanks

Since our problems have
been our own creation,
they also can be overcome.

George Harrison

To create one's own
world in any of the arts
takes courage.

Georgia O'Keefe

The worst is that the very
hardest thinking will not
bring thoughts. They must
come like good children
of God and cry, 'Here we are'.
You expend effort and
energy thinking hard. Then,
after you have given up,
they come sauntering in with
their hands in their pockets.
If the effort had not been
made to open the door,
however, who knows when
they could have come.

Johann Wolfgang von Goethe

Curiosity will conquer
fear even more than
bravery will.

James Stephens

The difficulty lies not
so much in developing
new ideas as in escaping
from old ones.

John Maynard Keynes

Transformative art
must express something
beyond where you are,
it demands that you grow
beyond your current self.
This is where an artist's
angst and the pain of
transformation coincide.
You reach toward the true,
the good and the beautiful
and become a better person
through the struggle.

Alex Grey

We work in the dark, we give what we have. Our doubt is our passion, and our passion is our task. The rest is the madness of art.

Henry James

I am irritated by my own writing. I am like a violinist whose ear is true, but whose fingers refuse to reproduce precisely the sound he hears within.

Gustave Flaubert

Even when I have to write a simple letter I'm scared stiff, as if faced with looming seasickness.

Gustav Klimt

The cave you fear
to enter holds the
treasure you seek.

Joseph Campbell

We do not believe in ourselves until someone reveals that deep inside us something is valuable, worth listening to, worthy of our trust, sacred to our touch. Once we believe in ourselves we can risk curiosity, wonder, spontaneous delight or any experience that reveals the human spirit.

E. E. Cummings

Talent is extremely common. What is rare is the willingness to endure the life of the writer.

Kurt Vonnegut

The worst enemy to creativity is self-doubt.

Sylvia Plath

I believe that adversity and negativity can be an amazing fuel towards personal success.

Jonathan Adler

It may be that the deep necessity of art is the examination of self-deception.

Robert Motherwell

Don't think about making art, just get it done. Let everyone else decide if it's good or bad, whether they love it or hate it. While they are deciding, make even more art.

Andy Warhol

Man's creative struggle, his search for wisdom and truth, is a love story.

Iris Murdoch

Painting is a source of endless pleasure, but also of great anguish.

Balthus

The mystery of creation works this way: We work and plan and break our backs for it. And then, in the ashes of our struggle, it appears like a gentle wind rustling through blades of grass. To find it seems impossible and yet, once here, it is as if it has always been this way.

Michael Jones

Most of the important things in the world have been accomplished by people who have kept on trying when there seemed to be no hope at all.

Dale Carnegie

Creativity is so delicate a flower that praise tends to make it bloom, while discouragement often nips it in the bud. Any of us will put out more and better ideas if our efforts are appreciated.

Alexander Osborn

Lipstick is the red badge of courage.

Man Ray

Creativity takes courage.

Henri Matisse

A picture should be a re-creation of an event rather than an illustration of an object; but there is no tension in the picture unless there is a struggle with the object.

Francis Bacon

Creativity is essentially a lonely art. An even lonelier struggle. To some a blessing. To others a curse. It is in reality the ability to reach inside yourself and drag forth from your very soul an idea.

Lou Dorfsman

I've had a million setbacks along the way – from kiln fires burning down buildings to shipping disasters – that should have put me out of business, or at least left me lying in the fetal position on my bed for a few days. Luckily, though, I've never for one second thought that I had any other option than to just keep going.

Jonathan Adler

It is all very well, when
the pen flows, but then there
are the dark days when
imagination deserts one, and
it is an effort to put anything
down on paper. That little
you have achieved stares at
you at the end of the day, and
you know the next morning
you will have to scrape it
down and start again.

Elizabeth Aston

SO YOU SEE, IMAGINATION NEEDS MOODLING – LONG, INEFFICIENT, HAPPY IDLING, DAWDLING AND PUTTERING.

Brenda Ueland

I AM A SIMPLE MAN, AND I USE SIMPLE MATERIALS: IVORY, BLACK, ETC. AND NO MEDIUM. THAT'S ALL I'VE EVER USED FOR MY PAINTING. I LIKE OILS. WATERCOLOURS I'VE USED ONLY OCCASIONALLY. THEY REALLY DON'T SUIT ME ... DRY TOO QUICKLY. THEY'RE NOT FLEXIBLE ENOUGH. I LIKE A MEDIUM YOU CAN WORK INTO, OVER A PERIOD OF TIME. THAT'S ABOUT ALL THERE IS TO SAY ON HOW I WORK.

L.S. Lowry

For the writer his vocabulary. For the pianist his piano. For the draughtsman a stick of graphite. Heaven and hell in a cedar tunnel. The scope is total. This is the first thing to realise. You have a rich, exhaustive medium capable of a thousand moods that lie between delicacy and violence. Increase or ease the pressure to your purpose. Explore its gamut and select your strength.

Mervyn Peake

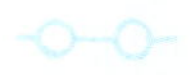

The painting has a life of its own. I try to let it come through.

Jackson Pollock

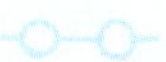

I avoid general anxiety by focusing on the process of painting, not the end result.

Linda Blondheim

Art is never finished, only abandoned.

Leonardo da Vinci

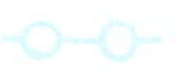

The longer you look at an object, the more abstract it becomes and, ironically, the more real.

Lucian Freud

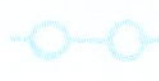

The promptitude with which many painters, on arriving at an entirely new and unfamiliar place, settle down to work at once, never fails to astonish me: it seems indecent, like button-holing a complete stranger.

Augustus John

If it takes more than five minutes, it's not graffiti.

Mint & Serf

JUST TO PAINT IS GREAT FUN. THE COLOURS ARE LOVELY TO LOOK AT AND DELICIOUS TO SQUEEZE OUT. MATCHING THEM, HOWEVER CRUDELY, WITH WHAT YOU SEE IS FASCINATING AND ABSOLUTELY ABSORBING.

Winston Churchill

ONE DOES NOT SET OUT WITH THE IDEA THAT I'VE JUST HAD A GREAT IDEA AND NOW I'M GOING TO GO AND CARRY IT OUT. ALMOST ALL ART THAT'S MADE LIKE THAT DOESN'T GO ANYWHERE.

Anish Kapoor

NEVER STATE A PROBLEM TO YOURSELF IN THE SAME TERMS AS IT WAS BROUGHT TO YOU.

Tom Hirshfield

WRITING IS EASY. ALL YOU HAVE TO DO IS CROSS OUT THE WRONG WORDS.

Mark Twain

I BACK AWAY FROM CONSCIOUS THOUGHT AND TURN THE PROBLEM OVER TO MY UNCONSCIOUS MIND. IT WILL SCAN A BROADER ARRAY OF PATTERNS AND FIND SOME NEW CLOSE FITS FROM OTHER INFORMATION STORED IN MY BRAIN.

Art Fry

AND SO A PICTURE EMERGES
THAT MAY LOOK QUITE GOOD FOR
A WHILE, SO AIRY AND COLOURFUL
AND NEW. BUT THAT WILL ONLY
LAST FOR A DAY AT MOST,
AT WHICH POINT IT STARTS TO
LOOK CHEAP AND FAKE. AND THEN
THE REAL WORK BEGINS – CHANGING,
ERADICATING, STARTING AGAIN,
AND SO ON, UNTIL IT'S DONE.

Gerhard Richter

THE SEED OF YOUR NEXT ARTWORK LIES EMBEDDED IN THE IMPERFECTIONS OF YOUR CURRENT PIECE.

David Bayles

THE ABILITY TO SIMPLIFY MEANS TO ELIMINATE THE UNNECESSARY SO THAT THE NECESSARY MAY SPEAK.

Hans Hofmann

It is part of the photographer's job to see more intensely than most people do. He must have and keep in him something of the receptiveness of the child who looks at the world for the first time or of the traveller who enters a strange country.

Bill Brandt

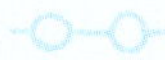

It seems reasonable to expect that beauty will emerge from a fusion of the individual character and culture of the potter, with the nature of his materials.

Bernard Leach

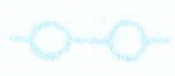

A certain amount of contempt for the material employed to express an idea is indispensable to the purest realization of this idea.

Man Ray

We try not to have ideas, preferring accidents. To create, you must empty yourself of every thought.

Gilbert & George

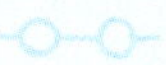

i do not put Collers what do not Belong. I Think it spoils The pictures. There have Been a lot of paintins spoiled By putin Collers where They do not Blong.

Alfred Wallis

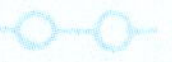

I never work with an audience – I can't do this. The process depends on the highest degree of nervous concentration.

Frank Auerbach

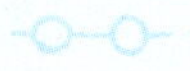

Sometimes when you're drunk you can see better.

Damien Hirst

I'M NOT INTERESTED IN PAINTING; I'M NOT INTERESTED IN MAKING A PICTURE. THEN WHAT THE HELL AM I INTERESTED IN? I MUST BE INTERESTED IN THIS PROCESS.

Philip Guston

WHEN I START TO PAINT, IT IS REAL AGONY. I GET NERVOUS. THE DAY BEFORE, I AM ALREADY WORKING UP TO IT. THEN I GET TO THE STUDIO AND, ONCE THE IMAGE STARTS TO EMERGE AND COME TOGETHER, PLEASURE KICKS IN. AND THEN YOU CAN SEE THINGS THAT NO OTHER PERSON CAN SEE.

Luc Tuymans

TAKE THE OBVIOUS, ADD
A CUPFUL OF BRAINS,
A GENEROUS PINCH OF
IMAGINATION, A BUCKETFUL
OF COURAGE AND DARING,
STIR WELL AND
BRING TO A BOIL.

Bernard Mannes Baruch

PAINTING IS MANUAL LABOUR,
NO DIFFERENT FROM ANY OTHER;
IT CAN BE DONE WELL OR POORLY.

George Grosz

I DESTROY THINGS EVERY DAY IN THE
ACT OF WORKING AND OFTEN RECALL
A PICTURE I HAD CONSIDERED FINISHED
IN ORDER TO REWORK IT.

Frank Auerbach

I CERTAINLY DO NOT BEGIN WITH ANY MEANING. IT IS AS THOUGH MY HANDS DO ALL THE THINKING.

Quentin Bell

I MUST ALWAYS HAVE A CLEAR IMAGE OF THE FORM OF A WORK BEFORE I BEGIN. OTHERWISE THERE IS NO IMPULSE TO CREATE.

Barbara Hepworth

IN THE CREATIVE STATE A MAN IS TAKEN OUT OF HIMSELF. HE LETS DOWN AS IT WERE A BUCKET INTO HIS SUBCONSCIOUS, AND DRAWS UP SOMETHING WHICH IS NORMALLY BEYOND HIS REACH. HE MIXES THIS THING WITH HIS NORMAL EXPERIENCES AND OUT OF THE MIXTURE HE MAKES A WORK OF ART.

E. M. Forster

THIS IS HOW YOU DO IT: YOU SIT DOWN AT THE KEYBOARD AND YOU PUT ONE WORD AFTER ANOTHER UNTIL IT'S DONE. IT'S THAT EASY, AND THAT HARD.

Neil Gaiman

I throw down the gauntlet to chance. For example, I prepare the ground for a picture by cleaning my brush over the canvas. Spilling a little turpentine can also be helpful.

Joan Miró

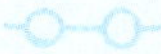

The painter can and must abstract from many details in creating his painting. Every good composition is above all a work of abstraction. All good painters know this. But the painter cannot dispense with subjects altogether without his work suffering impoverishment.

Diego Rivera

I have yet to see any problem, however complicated, which, when you looked at it in the right way, did not become still more complicated.

P.T. Anderson

There is nothing like looking, if you want to find something. You certainly usually find something, if you look, but it is not always quite the something you were after.

J.R.R. Tolkein

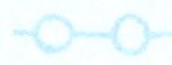

The faster I write the better my output. If I'm going slow, I'm in trouble. It means I'm pushing the words instead of being pulled.

Raymond Chandler

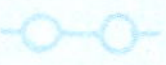

Any word you have to hunt for in a thesaurus is the wrong word.

Stephen King

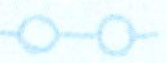

Get it down. Take chances. It may be bad, but it's the only way you can do anything really good.

William Faulkner

ONLY NOW I'M LEARNING TO ENJOY NOT BEING IN CHARGE OF WHAT THE NEXT STROKE WILL DO TO THE WHOLE PAINTING. I'M STILL LEARNING THAT THERE ARE NO MISTAKES, ONLY DISCOVERIES.

Fernando Araujo

MUDDY WATER IS BEST CLEARED
BY LEAVING IT ALONE.

Alan Watts

GREAT THINGS ARE DONE BY
A SERIES OF SMALL THINGS
BROUGHT TOGETHER.

Vincent van Gogh

PATIENCE IS ALSO A FORM OF ACTION.

Auguste Rodin

HALF OF WHAT I WRITE IS GARBAGE, BUT IF I DON'T WRITE IT DOWN IT DECOMPOSES IN MY HEAD.

Jarod Kintz

IDEALLY, ONE SHOULD HAVE MORE MATERIAL THAN ONE CAN POSSIBLY COPE WITH.

Frank Auerbach

ALL WRITERS HAVE THIS VAGUE HOPE THAT THE ELVES WILL COME IN THE NIGHT AND FINISH ANY STORIES.

Neil Gaiman

Don't get discouraged because there's a lot of mechanical work to writing. There is, and you can't get out of it. I rewrote the first part of *A Farewell to Arms* at least fifty times. You've got to work it over. The first draft of anything is shit. When you first start to write you get all the kick and the reader gets none, but after you learn to work it's your object to convey everything to the reader so that he remembers it not as a story he had read but something that happened to himself.

Ernest Hemingway

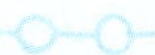

All the best performers bring to their role something more, something different than what the author put on paper. That's what makes theatre live. That's why it persists.

Stephen Sondheim

If the individual is narrowly concentrated on the goal, to the exclusion of other relevant aspects of the problem situation, he is often unable to achieve a solution. The creative thinker must stand sufficiently detached from his work.

Mary Henle

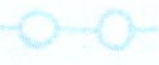

If there's ever a problem, I film it and it's no longer a problem. It's a film.

Andy Warhol

Intuition is the supra-logic that cuts out all the routine processes of thought and leaps straight from the problem to the answer.

Robert Graves

IT IS LOOKING AT THINGS FOR A LONG TIME THAT RIPENS YOU AND GIVES YOU A DEEPER UNDERSTANDING.

Vincent van Gogh

THAT'S THE TERRIBLE THING: THE MORE ONE WORKS ON A PICTURE, THE MORE IMPOSSIBLE IT BECOMES TO FINISH IT.

Alberto Giacometti

NO GREAT THING IS CREATED SUDDENLY, ANY MORE THAN A BUNCH OF GRAPES OR A FIG. IF YOU TELL ME THAT YOU DESIRE A FIG, I ANSWER YOU THAT THERE MUST BE TIME. LET IT FIRST BLOSSOM, THEN BEAR FRUIT, THEN RIPEN.

Epictetus

WHEN A PAINTER IS WORKING HE IS AWARE OF THE MEANS WHICH ARE AVAILABLE TO HIM — THESE INCLUDE HIS MATERIALS, THE STYLE HE INHERITS, THE CONVENTIONS HE MUST OBEY, HIS PRESCRIBED OR FREELY CHOSEN SUBJECT MATTER — AS CONSTITUTING BOTH AN OPPORTUNITY AND A RESTRAINT.

John Berger

IF I SET OUT TO SCULPT A STANDING MAN AND IT BECOMES A LYING WOMAN, I KNOW I AM MAKING ART.

Henry Moore

THE ENEMY OF ART IS THE ABSENCE OF LIMITATIONS.

Orson Welles

ALMOST ALL CREATIVITY REQUIRES PURPOSEFUL PLAY.

Abraham Maslow

AN ARTIST IS ATTRACTED TO CERTAIN KINDS OF FORM WITHOUT KNOWING WHY. YOU ADOPT A POSITION INTUITIVELY: ONLY LATER DO YOU ATTEMPT TO RATIONALISE OR EVEN JUSTIFY IT.

Fernando Botero

DESIGN IS NOT MAKING BEAUTY, BEAUTY EMERGES FROM SELECTION, AFFINITIES, INTEGRATION, LOVE.

Louis Kahn

PEOPLE WHO DO A JOB THAT CLAIMS TO BE CREATIVE HAVE TO BE ALONE TO RECHARGE THEIR BATTERIES. YOU CAN'T LIVE 24 HOURS A DAY IN THE SPOTLIGHT AND REMAIN CREATIVE. FOR PEOPLE LIKE ME, SOLITUDE IS A VICTORY.

Karl Lagerfeld

MENTAL DISCIPLINE OF DIRECTING AND CHOOSING ONES THOUGHTS, OF LETTING GO OF THE ONES THAT DO NOT SERVE THE PROCESS IS OF UTMOST IMPORTANCE.

Helena Tiainen

IT DOESN'T MATTER HOW THE PAINT IS PUT ON, AS LONG AS SOMETHING IS SAID.

Jackson Pollock

Artists are like the Phoenix, they periodically have to self-immolate, burn off an aspect of themselves to give birth to something new. The blank canvas demands you exceed yourself. And most times you fail. This pisses you off so bad you want to quit making art or makes some artists want to quit living. But then you calm down and come back to the work.

Alex Grey

I have found, for example, that if I have to write upon some rather difficult topic, the best plan is to think about it with very great intensity – the greatest intensity of which I am capable – for a few hours or days, and at the end of that time give orders, so to speak (to my subconscious mind) that the work is to proceed underground. After some months I return consciously to the topic and find that the work has been done.

Bertrand Russell

In order to create, we draw from our inner well. This inner well, an artistic reservoir, is ideally like a well stocked fish pond.... If we don't give some attention to upkeep, our well is apt to become depleted, stagnant, or blocked.... As artists, we must learn to be self nourishing. We must become alert enough to consciously replenish our creative resources as we draw on them – to restock the trout pond, so to speak.

Julia Cameron

If you get stuck, get away from your desk. Take a walk, take a bath, go to sleep, make a pie, draw, listen to music, meditate, exercise; whatever you do, don't just stick there scowling at the problem. But don't make telephone calls or go to a party; if you do, other people's words will pour in where your lost words should be. Open a gap for them, create a space. Be patient.

Hilary Mantel

WHEN I AM FINISHING A PICTURE, I HOLD SOME GOD-MADE OBJECT UP TO IT — A ROCK, A FLOWER, THE BRANCH OF A TREE OR MY HAND — AS A FINAL TEST. IF THE PAINTING STANDS UP BESIDE A THING MAN CANNOT MAKE, THE PAINTING IS AUTHENTIC. IF THERE'S A CLASH BETWEEN THE TWO, IT'S BAD ART.

Marc Chagall

STARTING TO PAINT, I FELT GLORIOUSLY FREE, QUIET, AND ALONE.

Henri Matisse

TO DRAW, YOU MUST CLOSE YOUR EYES AND SING.

Pablo Picasso

THE SCARIEST MOMENT IS ALWAYS JUST BEFORE YOU START.

Stephen King

Inspiration exists, but it has to find you working.

Pablo Picasso

A WORK OF ART IS NOT A MATTER OF THINKING BEAUTIFUL THOUGHTS OR EXPERIENCING TENDER EMOTIONS (THOUGH THOSE ARE ITS RAW MATERIALS), BUT OF INTELLIGENCE, SKILL, TASTE, PROPORTION, KNOWLEDGE, DISCIPLINE AND INDUSTRY: ESPECIALLY DISCIPLINE.

Evelyn Waugh

Chance favours only the prepared mind.

Louis Pasteur

One must always draw, draw with the eyes, when one cannot draw with a pencil.

Balthus

The unfed mind devours itself.

Gore Vidal

YOU DON'T GET INTO THE MOOD TO CREATE – IT'S DISCIPLINE.

Twyla Tharp

WITHOUT WORK, ALL LIFE GOES ROTTEN. BUT WHEN WORK IS SOULLESS, LIFE STIFLES AND DIES.

Albert Camus

Creativity is a combination of discipline and childlike spirit.

Robert Greene

DO WE NOT FIND FREEDOM ALONG THE GUIDING LINES OF DISCIPLINE?

Yehudi Menuhin

I DON'T WAIT FOR MOODS. YOU ACCOMPLISH NOTHING IF YOU DO THAT. YOUR MIND MUST KNOW IT HAS GOT TO GET DOWN TO WORK.

Pearl S. Buck

Just as appetite comes by eating, so work brings inspiration, if inspiration is not discernable at the beginning.

Igor Stravinsky

TALENT WITHOUT DISCIPLINE IS LIKE AN OCTOPUS ON ROLLER SKATES. THERE'S PLENTY OF MOVEMENT, BUT YOU NEVER KNOW IF IT'S GOING TO BE FORWARD, BACKWARDS OR SIDEWAYS.

H. Jackson Brown, Jr.

I CAN FIX A BAD PAGE. I CAN'T FIX A BLANK PAGE.

Nora Roberts

Discipline in art is a fundamental struggle to understand oneself, as much as to understand what one is drawing.

Henry Moore

Work inspires inspiration. Keep working. If you succeed, keep working. If you fail, keep working. If you're interested, keep working. If you're bored, keep working.

Michael Crichton

Your work is to discover your work and then with all your heart to give yourself up to it.

Gautama Buddha

The truth and beauty of line and form which by the slightest touch or twist of the brush a real artist imparts to every feature of his design must be founded on long, hard, persevering apprenticeship and a practice so habitual that it has become instinctive.

Winston Churchill

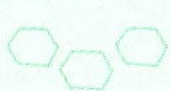

All of those art-based fields are similar in that they're all hard to make a living in and they all require an intense amount of training and discipline.

Alicia Witt

I go out each morning and draw. I can't really start a painting in the morning until I've done a drawing.

Frank Auerbach

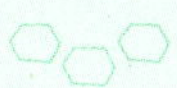

Writing is like breathing, it's possible to learn to do it well, but the point is to do it no matter what.

Julia Cameron

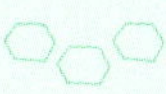

Inspiration comes and goes, creativity is the result of practice.

Phil Cousineau

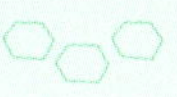

Painting is a self-disciplined activity that you have to learn by yourself.

Romare Bearden

TALK OF INSPIRATION IS SHEER NONSENSE: THERE IS NO SUCH THING. IT IS MERELY A MATTER OF CRAFTSMANSHIP.

William Morris

YOU MUST BE PREPARED TO WORK ALWAYS WITHOUT APPLAUSE.

Ernest Hemingway

YOU WILL SUCCEED BECAUSE MOST PEOPLE ARE LAZY.

Shahir Zag

RESIST MUCH. OBEY LITTLE.

Walt Whitman

I DON'T BELIEVE IN INSPIRATION. I BELIEVE IN WORK, BECAUSE WHILE ONE WORKS ONE'S CREATIVITY IS OPENED.

Giacomo Manzù

Luck is what happens when preparation meets opportunity.

Seneca

Talent is cheap: dedication is expensive. It will cost you your life.

Irving Stone

I paint every day. Sometimes I hate painting, but I keep at it, thinking always that before I croak I'll really learn how to do it – maybe as well as some of the old painters.

Thomas Hart Benton

I'll have periods when I write and periods when I don't. But you don't want it to become a discipline, really. If it becomes a discipline, it becomes a chore, and that's no good. To make art you need to be inspired.

Greg Lake

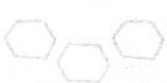

True freedom is impossible without a mind made free by discipline.

Mortimer J. Adler

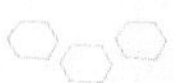

On Willem de Kooning ...
Like bodies, these canvases are subject to both discipline and incontinence, to the utmost athletic control, and to fumbles, spurts, accidents.

Andrew Forge

There is just now a great clamour and demand for 'culture' but it is not so much culture that is needed as discipline.

William Shedd

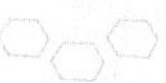

It is one thing to praise discipline, and another to submit to it.

Miguel de Cervantes

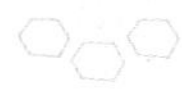

What is before me and what is inside of me governs all.

Henry Casselli

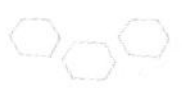

Creativity is a wild mind and a disciplined eye.

Dorothy Parker

There is no time for cut-and-dried monotony. There is time for work. And time for love. That leaves no other time.

Coco Chanel

A lot of people talk about writing. The secret is to write, not talk.

Jackie Collins

Stare. It is the way to educate your eye, and more. Stare, pry, listen, eavesdrop. Die knowing something. You are not here long.

Walker Evans

People say, 'What a discipline, painting so much.' I say, 'No, I love it.' Nothing amuses me as much as my work. To have discipline would be **not** to paint.

Fernando Botero

CREATIVE THINKING – IN TERMS OF IDEA CREATIVITY – IS NOT A MYSTICAL TALENT. IT IS A SKILL THAT CAN BE PRACTISED AND NURTURED.

Edward de Bono

It is essential ... that discipline should not be practised like a rule imposed on oneself from the outside, but that it becomes an expression of one's own will; that it is felt as pleasant, and that one slowly accustoms oneself to a kind of behaviour which one would eventually miss, if one stopped practising it.

Erich Fromm

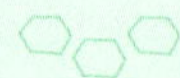

Art is the only discipline where saying less means more.

Andrew Hamilton

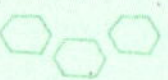

An artist's fine goal is to manifest a well-nigh heroic self-discipline, carefully attending to all that concerns him.

Eric Maisel

Study the science of art. Study the art of science. Develop your senses – especially learn how to see. Realise that everything connects to everything else.

Leonardo da Vinci

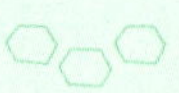

Problems, however, are rarely solved on the spur of the moment. They must be organized and dissected, then key issues isolated and defined. A period of gestation then sets in, during which these issues are mulled over. You put them in your mind and consciously or unconsciously work at them at odd hours of the day or night – even at work. It is somewhat analogous to trying to place a name on the face of someone you've met before. Often the solution to a problem comes to you in much the same way you eventually recall the name.

Bill Hewlett

One factor that makes a good and successful artist, is discipline. It's the essence of the whole thing. And sadly, many young artists today lack that quality.

Irwin Greenberg

DISCIPLINE IS ADMIRED IN OPERA SINGERS, ENGINEERS, DANCERS, PIANISTS OR BRAIN SURGEONS BUT, FOR SOME PECULIAR REASON, WHEN A PAINTER IS UNDISCIPLINED, IT IS CONSIDERED CREATIVE, NEW AND INNOVATIVE, OR EVEN GENIUS. USUALLY, IT IS JUST BAD PAINTING.

Patricia Moran

Art is work like any other discipline, and most artists and would-be artists and art lovers need to realise that.

Heidi Hehn

The only person who can pull me down is myself, and I'm not going to let myself pull me down anymore.

C. Joybell C.

I BELIEVE EVERYBODY IS CREATIVE, AND EVERYBODY IS TALENTED. I JUST DON'T THINK THAT EVERYBODY IS DISCIPLINED. I THINK THAT'S A RARE COMMODITY.

Al Hershfeld

IF YOU WANT TO CHANGE YOUR ART, CHANGE YOUR HABITS.

Clement Greenberg

We artists tend to be lone wolves in our work. No one tells us to go to the studio. We just go.... The work itself is a quiet pursuit, alone in the studio or on site.... And that takes discipline.

Jackie Knott

Hours of preparation for something that is excecuted, with extreme precision, in a few minutes. Just as with a judo throw.

Yves Klein

It's so easy to be undisciplined. And to be disciplined is so against my character, my general nature anyway, that I have to strain a little bit to keep on the right track.

Robert Rauschenberg

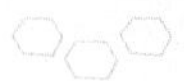

It is far more difficult to be simple than to be complicated; far more difficult to sacrifice skill and easy execution in the proper place, than to expand both indiscriminately.

John Ruskin

The most demanding part of living a lifetime as an artist is the strict discipline of forcing oneself to work steadfastly along the nerve of one's own intimate sensitivity.

Anne Truitt

Those who are waiting for an epiphany to strike may wait forever. The artist simply goes to work, making art, both good and not so good.

Chuck Close

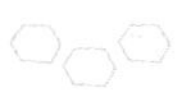

Pottery for me is not a pursuit of glory, but a daily discipline of pursuing accuracy. In India it would be called my Dharma. Life is dual. There is matter and spirit and one cannot function completely without the other. For creativity, the spirit side, to work, the matter side must be strong enough to hold the spirit side. If the form has cracks, the spirit leaks.

Beatrice Wood

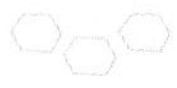

The price of excellence is discipline. The cost of mediocrity is disappointment.

William Arthur Ward

LEARN THE RULES LIKE A PRO, SO YOU CAN BREAK THEM LIKE AN ARTIST.

Pablo Picasso

WORK ON PURPOSE – PLAY ON PURPOSE – REST ON PURPOSE. DO NOT LET YOURSELF OR ANYONE ELSE WASTE YOUR TIME.

Izey Victoria Odiase

In art, truth and reality begin when one no longer understands what one is doing or what one knows, and when there remains an energy that is all the stronger for being constrained, controlled and compressed.

Henri Matisse

If I try my best and fail, well, I've tried my best.

Steve Jobs

There is no art which has not had its beginnings in things full of errors. Nothing is at the same time both new and perfect.

Leon Battista Alberti

Men stumble over pebbles, never over mountains.

Anonymous

Success is not final, failure is not fatal. It's the courage to continue that counts

Winston Churchill

Artists know failure. It is not tragic that they know failure; it is only tragic if they know failure and little else...

Eric Maisel

If you get up one more time than you fall down, you will make it through

Chinese proverb

To copy oneself is more dangerous than to copy others. It leads to sterility.

Pablo Picasso

The minute you start thinking about what you're going to do if you lose, you have lost.

George P. Schultz

In nature everything is always right: the structure is right, the proportions are good, the colours fit the forms. If you imitate that in painting, it becomes false.

Gerhard Richter

I don't feel any real animosity towards critics when they write negative things. I think some are more perceptive than others. Some are very knowledgeable about painting. But it isn't something I have any influence over, so there isn't any point in worrying about it.

Peter Doig

I'm proof against that word failure. I've seen behind it. The only failure a man ought to fear is failure of cleaving to the purpose he sees to be best.

George Eliot

Finish each day and be done with it. You have done what you could. Some blunders and absurdities have crept in – forget them as soon as you can. Tomorrow is a new day. You shall begin it serenely and with too high a spirit to be encumbered with your old nonsense.

Ralph Waldo Emerson

I assumed that everything would lead to complete failure, but I decided that didn't matter – that would be my life.

Jasper Johns

If you get a bad review, you take that in your stride.

Anish Kapoor

It is precisely from the regret left by the imperfect work that the next one can be born.

Odilon Redon

An artist's failures are as valuable as his successes: by misjudging one thing he conforms something else, even if at the time he does not know what that something else is.

Brigit Riley

A real failure does not need an excuse. It is an end in itself.

Gertrude Stein

Artistic failure may be labours lost but is life lived.

Ian Semple

Nothing is a waste of time if you use the experience wisely.

Auguste Rodin

I have not failed once. I've just found 10,000 ways that didn't work.

Thomas A. Edison

If at first you don't succeed, try, try again. Then quit. No use being a damn fool about it.

W.C. Fields

An artist, a man, a failure,
must proceed.
E.E. Cummings

If at first you don't succeed,
failure may be your style.
Quentin Crisp

Develop success from failures.
Discouragement and
failure are two of the surest
stepping stones to success.
Dale Carnegie

Many of life's failures are
people who did not realize
how close they were to
success when they gave up.
Thomas A. Edison

Failures are events,
not people.
Grace Duck

Failure is unimportant.
It takes courage to make
a fool of yourself.
Charlie Chaplin

It's better to fail in
originality, than succeed
in imitation.
Herman Melville

Can anything be sadder
than work left unfinished?
Yes, work never begun.
Christina Rossetti

My life is full of mistakes.
They're like pebbles that
make a good road.

Beatrice Wood

A love of nature is a consolation
against failure.

Berthe Morisot

Give me the young man who has brains enough to make a fool of himself.

Robert Louis Stevenson

You may be disappointed if you fail, but you are doomed if you don't try.

Beverly Sills

When we can begin to take our failures non-seriously, it means we are ceasing to be afraid of them. It is of immense importance to laugh at ourselves.

Katherine Mansfield

You may have a fresh start any moment you choose, for this thing that we call 'failure' is not the falling down, but the staying down.

Mary Pickford

Never confuse a single defeat with a final defeat.

F. Scott Fitzgerald

The world is divided into two categories: failures and unknowns.

Frances Picabia

Ever tried.

Ever failed.

No matter. Try again.

Fail Again.

Fail better.

Samuel Beckett

The only real failure is trying to second-guess the taste of an audience. Nothing comes out of that except a kind of inward humiliation.
David Bowie

I failed my way to success. I am not discouraged, because every wrong attempt discarded is another step forward.
Thomas A. Edison

One inconvenience ... may attend bold and arduous attempts: frequent failure may discourage. This evil, however, is not more pernicious than the slow proficiency which is the natural consequence of too easy tasks.
Sir Joshua Reynolds

Fall seven times, stand up eight.
Japanese Proverb

I honestly think it is better to be a failure at something you love than to be a success at something you hate.
George Burns

The season of failure is the best time for sowing the seeds of success.
Paramahansa Yogananda

Failure is the condiment that gives success its flavor.
Truman Capote

I know very well what I am about and that my skies have not been neglected, though they often failed in execution – and often no doubt from over anxiety about them....

John Constable

Most of my conscious efforts have ended in embarrassing failure....

Ingmar Bergman

I had to come to terms with my failure as an artist … I had to find a way for myself.

Tracey Emin

He who is discouraged after a failure is not a real artist.

Auguste Rodin

An artist cannot fail; it is a success to be one.

Charles Horton Cooley

Do not fear mistakes.
There are none.

Miles Davis

Failure is only the opportunity to begin again more intelligently.

Henry Ford

Act as if it were impossible to fail.

Dorothea Brande

By the time I was fourteen the nail in my wall would no longer support the weight of the rejection slips impaled upon it. I replaced the nail with a spike and went on writing.

Stephen King

I have no fears about making changes, destroying the image … because the painting has a life of its own. I try to let it come through. It is only when I lose contact with the painting that the result is a mess.

Jackson Pollock

The goal in life is to be solid, whereas the way that life works is totally fluid, so you can never actually achieve that goal.

Damian Hirst

A man can fail many times, but he isn't a failure until he begins to blame somebody else.

John Burroughs

To try and fail is at least to learn. To fail to try is to suffer the loss of what might have been.

Benjamin Franklin

Failure is a bruise, not a tatoo.

Jon Sinclair

Creativity is allowing yourself to make mistakes. Art is knowing which ones to keep.

Scott Adams

Failure is the path of least persistence.

Anonymous

Mistakes are almost always of a sacred nature. Never try to correct them. On the contrary: rationalize them, understand them thoroughly. After that, it will be possible for you to sublimate them.

Salvador Dalí

Above all, it's hard learning to live with vivid mental images of scenes I cared for and failed to photograph. It is the edgy existence within me of these unmade images that is the only assurance that the best photographs are yet to be made.

Sam Abell

Most success springs from an obstacle or failure. I became a cartoonist largely because I failed in my goal of becoming a successful executive.

Scott Adams

They who have conquered doubt and fear have conquered failure.

James Allen

If you're not failing every now and again, it's a sign you're not doing anything very innovative.

Woody Allen

There is no such thing as a failed painting, there is only practise for a successful one ... as long as there are artists who paint better than I do, I will remain a student. I expect to die a student.

Brenda Behr

Without fail, three or four hideous paintings down the road, an absolutely wonderful painting appears. A painting that is a better painting than I know how to do. A painting that feels effortless.

Eleanor Blair

You have to learn how to accept rejection, and reject acceptance.

Ray Bradbury

There is nothing worse than a brilliant image of a fuzzy concept.

Ansel Adams

Mistakes are the portals of discovery.

James Joyce

No matter how well you perform, there's always somebody of intelligent opinion who thinks it's lousy.

Sir Laurence Olivier

THE ONLY PLACE WHERE SUCCESS COMES BEFORE WORK IS IN THE DICTIONARY.

Vidal Sassoon

SUCCESS AND FAILURE ARE BOTH DIFFICULT TO ENDURE. ALONG WITH SUCCESS COME DRUGS, DIVORCE, FORNICATION, BULLYING, TRAVEL, MEDITATION, MEDICATION, DEPRESSION, NEUROSIS AND SUICIDE. WITH FAILURE COMES FAILURE.

Joseph Heller

There was a reviewer ... who wrote that my pictures didn't have any beginning or any end. He didn't mean it as a compliment, but it was. It was a fine compliment.

Jackson Pollock

Whenever I got a new studio I made the largest possible painting, and since the ceiling was low, the painting became horizontal. As I changed studios and got larger spaces, I made bigger paintings.

James Rosenquist

Art is exalted above religion and race. Not a single solitary soul these days believes in the religions of the Assyrians, the Egyptians and the Greeks... Only their art, whenever it was beautiful, stands proud and exalted, rising above all time.

Emil Nolde

He has achieved success
who has lived well, laughed
often, and loved much;
Who has enjoyed the trust
of pure women, the respect
of intelligent men and the
love of little children;
Who has filled his niche
and accomplished his task;
Who has never lacked
appreciation of Earth's
beauty or failed to express it;
Who has left the world
better than he found it,
Whether an improved
poppy, a perfect poem,
or a rescued soul;
Who has always looked for
the best in others and given
them the best he had;
Whose life was an inspiration;
Whose memory a benediction.

Bessie Anderson Stanley

Success is a consequence and must not be a goal.

Gustave Flaubert

IF YOU EVER FIND THAT YOU'RE THE MOST TALENTED PERSON IN THE ROOM, YOU NEED TO FIND ANOTHER ROOM.

Austin Kleon

SUCCESS IS COUNTED SWEETEST /
BY THOSE WHO NE'ER SUCCEED. /
TO COMPREHEND A NECTAR /
REQUIRES SOREST NEED.

Emily Dickinson

IT HAD LONG SINCE COME TO MY ATTENTION THAT PEOPLE OF ACCOMPLISHMENT RARELY SAT BACK AND LET THINGS HAPPEN TO THEM. THEY WENT OUT AND HAPPENED TO THINGS.

Leonardo da Vinci

ASK YOURSELF THE SECRET OF YOUR SUCCESS. LISTEN TO YOUR ANSWER, AND PRACTISE IT.

Richard Bach

YOU CAN LOOK AT A PAINTING FOR A WHOLE WEEK AND THEN NEVER THINK ABOUT IT AGAIN. YOU CAN ALSO LOOK AT A PAINTING FOR A SECOND AND THINK ABOUT IT FOR THE REST OF YOUR LIFE.

Joan Miró

GOOD ART SHOULD ELICIT A RESPONSE OF 'HUH? WOW!' AS OPPOSED TO 'WOW! HUH?'

Ed Ruscha

SUCCESS IS WHEN I'M OUT ON LOCATION AND CAN PULL OFF A DECENT PAINTING. IT'S ALSO WHEN I CAN CONVINCE SOMEONE WHO IS AFRAID, TO PUT BRUSH TO CANVAS AND FEEL THE JOY.

Linda Blondheim

WHAT COUNTS MOST IS FINDING NEW WAYS TO GET THE WORLD DOWN IN PAINT ON MY OWN TERMS.

Georg Baselitz

I WAS FEELING GUILTY IN THE BEGINNING; IT WAS FRUSTRATING TO BE SUCCESSFUL WHEN A LOT OF MY FRIENDS WEREN'T. ALSO, I WAS CONSTANTLY BEING REMINDED OF THAT BY PEOPLE IN MY FAMILY MAKING JOKES.

Cindy Sherman

THERE IS A KIND OF SUCCESS THAT IS INDISTINGUISHABLE FROM PANIC.

Edward Degas

THE TOUGHEST THING ABOUT SUCCESS IS THAT YOU HAVE GOT TO KEEP ON BEING A SUCCESS.

Irving Berlin

TO BE SUCCESSFUL YOU HAVE TO BE LUCKY, OR A LITTLE MAD, OR VERY TALENTED, OR FIND YOURSELF IN A RAPID GROWTH FIELD.

Edward de Bono

YOU LIKE IT, THAT'S ALL, WHETHER IT'S A LANDSCAPE OR ABSTRACT. YOU LIKE IT. IT HITS YOU. YOU DON'T HAVE TO READ IT.

Clement Greenberg

A minute's success pays the failure of years.

Robert Browning

Success is dangerous. One begins to copy oneself, and to copy oneself is more dangerous than to copy others.

Pablo Picasso

Whether you succeed or not is irrelevant, there is no such thing. Making your unknown known is the important thing

Georgia O'Keefe

There are only four words to success as a painter... paint, paint, paint, PAINT!

Laurel Cormack

The only thing you have to fear more than failure is success.

Ted Godwin

That's me, the twenty-five year overnight sensation.

Ed Ruscha

Letter to Vincent van Gogh, January 22, 1890:
I think we can wait patiently for success to come; you will surely live to see it. It is necessary to get well known without obtruding oneself, and it will come of its own accord by reason of your beautiful pictures.

Theo van Gogh

Success makes life easier. It doesn't make living easier.

Bruce Springsteen

FAIL I ALONE,
IN WORDS AND DEEDS?
WHY, ALL MEN
STRIVE AND
WHO SUCCEEDS?

Robert Browning

SUCCESS MUST COME GENTLY, WITH
A GREAT DEAL OF EFFORT BUT WITH
NO STRESS OR OBSESSION.

Carlos Castaneda

WE MUST BELIEVE IN LUCK.
FOR HOW ELSE CAN WE EXPLAIN THE
SUCCESS OF THOSE WE DON'T LIKE?

Jean Cocteau

SUCCESS IS A KIND OF PEACE OF MIND.

Kelly Borsheim

PICTURES MUST BE MIRACULOUS: THE INSTANT ONE IS COMPLETED, THE INTIMACY BETWEEN THE CREATION AND THE CREATOR IS ENDED.

Mark Rothko

SELF-TRUST IS THE FIRST SECRET TO SUCCESS.

Ralph Waldo Emerson

STYLE IS KNOWING WHO YOU ARE, WHAT YOU WANT TO SAY, AND NOT GIVING A DAMN.

Gore Vidal

I SUCCEEDED IN SIMPLY ATTENDING AT THE BIRTH OF ALL MY WORKS.

Max Ernst

TO ACCOMPLISH GREAT THINGS, WE MUST NOT ONLY ACT, BUT ALSO DREAM, NOT ONLY PLAN, BUT ALSO BELIEVE.

Anatole France

A MAN IS A SUCCESS IF HE GETS UP IN THE MORNING AND GETS TO BED AT NIGHT, AND IN BETWEEN HE DOES WHAT HE WANTS TO.

Bob Dylan

IT'S NOT WHERE YOU TAKE THINGS FROM – IT'S WHERE YOU TAKE THEM TO.

Jean Luc Godard

AN IDEAL TRANSACTION:
A PESSIMIST CREATES AN ART,
AN OPTIMIST BUYS IT.

Prakesh Ghai

CONQUER, BUT DON'T TRIUMPH.

Marie von Ebner-Eschenbach

WHEN ANY CREATIVITY BECOMES USEFUL, IT IS SUCKED INTO THE VORTEX OF COMMERCIALISM, AND WHEN A THING BECOMES COMMERCIAL, IT BECOMES THE ENEMY OF MAN.

Arthur Miller

IT IS GOOD TO LOVE MANY THINGS, FOR THEREIN LIES TRUE STRENGTH, AND WHOSOEVER LOVES MUCH PERFORMS MUCH, AND CAN ACCOMPLISH MUCH, AND WHAT IS DONE IN LOVE IS WELL DONE.

Vincent van Gogh

The artist ... standing in the position of mediator between the world of his experience and the world of his dreams – 'a mediator, consequently gifted with twin faculties, a selective faculty and a reproductive faculty'. To equate these faculties was the secret of artistic success.

James Joyce

Whosoever desires constant success must change his conduct with the times.

Niccolò Machiavelli

In most cases success equals prison... An artist should never be: prisoner of himself, prisoner of a manner, prisoner of a reputation, prisoner of success.

Henri Matisse

The worst part of success is to try finding someone who is happy for you.

Bette Midler

When women do succeed, the press, even the industry press, spend far too much time talking about how we dress, what shoes we're wearing, who we're meant to be seeing. That's pretty sad for women, especially when it's written by women who really should know better.

Zaha Hadid

As for myself, I met with as much success as I could ever have wanted. In other words, I was enthusiastically run-down by every critic of the period.

Claude Monet

DARING IDEAS ARE LIKE CHESSMEN MOVED FORWARD; THEY MAY BE BEATEN, BUT THEY MAY START A WINNING GAME.

Johann Wolfgang von Goethe

I WAS OBLIGED TO BE INDUSTRIOUS. WHOEVER IS EQUALLY INDUSTRIOUS WILL SUCCEED ... EQUALLY WELL.

Johann Sebastian Bach

THE NATURE OF THE MASTERPIECES IS NOT TO DAZZLE. THEIR NATURE IS TO PERSUADE, TO CONVINCE, TO ENTER INTO US THROUGH OUR PORES.

Jean-Auguste-Dominique Ingres

I KNOW THE PRICE OF SUCCESS: DEDICATION, HARD WORK AND AN UNREMITTING DEVOTION TO THE THINGS YOU WANT TO SEE HAPPEN.

Frank Lloyd Wright

I DREAD SUCCESS. TO HAVE SUCCEEDED IS TO HAVE FINISHED ONE'S BUSINESS ON EARTH, LIKE THE MALE SPIDER WHO IS KILLED BY THE FEMALE THE MOMENT HE HAS SUCCEEDED IN HIS COURTSHIP. I LIKE THE STATE OF CONTINUAL BECOMING, WITH A GOAL IN FRONT AND NOT BEHIND.

George Bernard Shaw

WHEN A SMALL CHILD, I THOUGHT THAT SUCCESS SPELLED HAPPINESS. I WAS WRONG, HAPPINESS IS LIKE A BUTTERFLY WHICH APPEARS AND DELIGHTS US FOR ONE BRIEF MOMENT, BUT SOON FLITS AWAY.

Anna Pavlova

SUCCESS IS RELATIVE: IT IS WHAT WE CAN MAKE OF THE MESS WE HAVE MADE OF THINGS.

T.S. Eliot

Now, more than ever,
I realise just how illusory
my undeserved success has
been. I still hold out some
hope of doing better, but
age and unhappiness have
sapped my strength.

Claude Monet

I don't think you ever
feel a success really
because everything could
always be done better
than you've done it....

John Mortimer

Success for an artist
is completed work.
Very successful artists
complete a lot of work.
It's that simple.

Paul Russo

Whether you succeed or
not is irrelevant, there is
no such thing.

Georgia O'Keeffe

I have arrived more
definitely than any other
painter during his lifetime;
honours shower upon me
from every side; artists pay
me compliments on my work;
there are many people to
whom my position must
seem enviable.... But
I don't seem to have a
single real friend!

Pierre-Auguste Renoir

Success is not greedy,
as people think, but
insignificant. That's why
it satisfies nobody.

Seneca

YOU HAVE TO BE BURNING WITH AN IDEA, OR A PROBLEM, OR A WRONG THAT YOU WANT TO RIGHT. IF YOU'RE NOT PASSIONATE ENOUGH FROM THE START, YOU'LL NEVER STICK IT OUT.

Steve Jobs

TALENT IS CHEAPER THAN TABLE SALT. WHAT SEPARATES THE TALENTED INDIVIDUAL FROM THE SUCCESSFUL ONE IS A LOT OF HARD WORK.

Stephen King

YOU'VE ACHIEVED SUCCESS IN YOUR FIELD WHEN YOU DON'T KNOW WHETHER WHAT YOU'RE DOING IS WORK OR PLAY.

Warren Beatty

THE GREATEST REWARD FOR A MAN'S TOIL IS NOT WHAT HE GETS BY IT, BUT WHAT HE BECOMES BY IT.

John Ruskin

SUCCESS IS BLOCKED BY CONCENTRATING ON IT AND PLANNING FOR IT. SUCCESS IS SHY – IT WON'T COME OUT WHILE YOU'RE WATCHING.

Tennessee Williams

As long as I have
a want, I have
a reason for living.
Satisfaction is death.

George Bernard Shaw

To be full of joy when
looking at an oeuvre
is not a little thing.

Hans Jean Arp

Making money is art
and working is art
and good business is
the best art of all.

Andy Warhol

Above all,
an artist must
never be too
easily satisfied
with what he
has done....

Henri Matisse

A man's life is his work;
his work is his life.

Jackson Pollock

Art is not to do
with the practical
side of making a living.
It's to live a fuller
human life.

Henry Moore

Even in the centuries which appear to us to be the most monstrous and foolish, the immortal appetite for beauty has always found satisfaction.

Charles Baudelaire

+

The greatest pleasure is not – say – sex or geometry. It is just understanding. And if you can get people to understand their own humanity – well, that's the job of the writer.

William Golding

+

The idea that one might derive satisfaction from his or her successful work, because that work is ingenious, beautiful, or just pleasing, has become ridiculed.

Niklaus Wirth

A negative judgment gives you more satisfaction than praise, provided it smacks of jealousy.

Jean Baudrillard

+

What exactly is success? For me it is to be found not in applause, but in the satisfaction of feeling that one is realising one's ideal.

Anna Pavlova

+

Show me a thoroughly satisfied man and I will show you a failure.

Thomas A. Edison

+

I'd rather be dead than singing 'Satisfaction' when I'm forty-five.

Mick Jagger

You've got to get up every morning with determination if you're going to go to bed with satisfaction.

George Lorimer

The artist's life is the best life ... if you can get through the first forty years.

Thomas Hart Benton

Since I am the
creator of the
painting and the
first real 'viewer'
– when I feel satisfied,
I put the brushes
down and hope that
someone else will feel
satisfied too.

David Lussier

Be satisfied with success in even the smallest matter, and think that even such a result is no trifle.

Marcus Aurelius

One day I am satisfied, the next day I find it all bad; still I hope that some day I will find some of them good....

Claude Monet

An artist paints, dances, draws, writes, designs or acts at the expanding edge of consciousness. We press into the unknown rather than the known. This makes life lovely and lively.

Julia Cameron

There is no
effect more
disproportionate
to its cause
than the
happiness
bestowed by
a small
compliment.

Robert Brault

If a painting of mine
suits me, it is right.
If it does not please
me, I care not if
all the great masters
should approve it
or the dealers buy it.
They would be wrong.

Arshile Gorky

One cannot demand of art that it pay you in any other way than in the satisfaction of the work itself.

Uta Hagen

Creation not destruction brings satisfaction and happiness.

Ian Massey

I longed to arrest
all beauty that came
before me, and at
length the longing
has been satisfied.

Julia Cameron

God was satisfied
with his own work,
and that is fatal.

Samuel Butler

It's the nicest
thing on earth
if someone comes
up to me and says,
'Every day I drink
out of a mug
you designed.'

Jonathan Adler

You have not
found your place
until all your faculties
are roused, and
your whole nature
consents and approves
of the work you
are doing.

Orison Swett Marden

Life is very short ...
but I would like
to live four times
and if I could,
I would set out
to do no other
things than I am
seeking now to do.

William Merritt Chase

Eventually the satisfaction gets greater with each effort.

William F. Reese

The noblest pleasure is the joy of understanding.

Leonardo da Vinci

If everybody was satisfied with himself, there would be no heroes.

Mark Twain

When I read it,
I don't wince, which
is all I ever ask for
a book I write.

Norman Mailer

I suppose what is
most gratifying to me
is the continual sense
of discovery in the painting
process, which is one of
change and adaptation.

Joan Ashley Evanescent

The true secret of
happiness lies in taking a
genuine interest in all the
details of daily life.

William Morris

It is not in life, but in art
that self-fulfilment
is to be found.

George E. Woodberry

The fulfillment
of being an artist ...
is in the doing,
or the 'joy of
process', and
the pleasure and
excitement of
striving for
perfection.

Suzy Smith

It is so easy to delude yourself that you have done a masterpiece! Each time you have to tell yourself, 'I've simply got to do better.'

Ken Flitton

Art is there for nourishment, not explication.

Walter Darby Bannard

Preparing for an exhibition in 2000, Jack Madson at last finished to his satisfaction an abstract painting he had begun in 1957. He did so by photographing the original piece, then reworking sections of it by first applying brush-strokes in miniature directly on top of the colour photo print, and finally, when he'd solved all of the problems, repainting those portions of the canvas. 'Time means nothing,' he said. 'You've got to get it right, until it looks like it does in your mind.'

Stewart Wachs on Jack Madson

+

I have always liked it, it is still my favourite book. I do not like my writing, but I like this book.... I wish I liked my own writing more, but like all of us, I am trapped inside my own skin.

William Golding

At times I come across works of mine which are soundly done and really in my style, and at such moments I find great solace.

Camille Pissarro

+

I have often, as an exercise and as a sustenance, painted before an object down to the smallest accidents of its visual appearance. But the day left me sad and with an unsatiated thirst. The next day I let the other source run, that of imagination through the recollection of the forms and I was then reassured and appeased.

Odilon Redon

+

The harder I work the more I live.

George Bernard Shaw

I'm not sure
what [my latest
works are] about
but I'm convinced
they're the best things
I've done and I'm
going to the world's
best museums
with them.

Mark Kostabi

One of life's most fulfilling moments occurs in that split second when the familiar is suddenly transformed into the dazzling aura of the profoundly new.

Joan Ashley Evanescent

Satisfaction lies in the effort, not in the attainment. Full effort is full victory.

Mahatma Ghandi

Everything is worth precisely as much as a belch, the difference being that a belch is more satisfying.

Ingmar Bergman

Do it right or don't do it at all. That comes from my mom. If there's something I want to do, I'm one of those people that won't be satisfied until I get it done.

Ray Charles

The only person you have to please, with your art, is yourself.

Don Getz

I get great satisfaction
in creating a visual oasis
to gaze at for a moment
of peaceful escape from
the turbulent world.

Evelyn Dayman

The fastidious are
unfortunate; nothing
satisfies them.

Jean de La Fontaine

There are
some days
when I think I'm
going to die from
an overdose
of satisfaction.

Salvador Dalí

I wished to copy nature. I could not. But I was satisfied when I discovered the sun, for instance, could not be reproduced, but only represented by something else.

Paul Cézanne

The critics can say stupid things and we can enjoy them, if we have the legitimate feeling of superiority – the satisfaction of a duty accomplished.

Paul Gauguin

A bellyful is a bellyful.

Francois Rebelais

Art, like morality, consists in drawing the line somewhere.

G.K. Chesterton

Life beats down and crushes the soul and art reminds you that you have one.

Stella Adler

Man needs music, literature, and painting – all those oases of perfection that make up art – to compensate for the rudeness and materialism of life.

Fernando Botero

Painting: The art of protecting flat surfaces from the weather and exposing them to the critic.

Ambrose Bierce

Every time I paint a portrait I lose a friend.

John Singer Sargent

There is no better deliverance from the world than through art; and a man can form no surer bond with it than through art.

Johann Wolfgang von Goethe

Creativity can solve almost any problem. The creative act, the defeat of habit by originality, overcomes everything.

George Lois

I force myself to contradict myself in order to avoid conforming to my own taste.

Marcel Duchamp

To keep from going stale, you must forget your professional outlook and rediscover the virginal eye of the amateur.

Brassai

Creative people have
an abiding curiosity and
an insatiable desire to learn
how and why things work.
They take nothing for granted.
They are interested in things
around them and tend to
stow away bits and pieces
of information in their minds
for future use. And,
they have a great ability
to mobilise their thinking
and experiences for use in
solving a new problem.

Bill Hewlett

You connect yourself to the
viewer by sharing something
that is inside of you that
connects with something
inside of him. All you have
as your guide is that you
know what moves you.

Steven Brust

The most beautiful thing
we can experience is the
mysterious. It is the source
of all true art and science.

Albert Einstein

Our species is the only
creative species, and it has
only one creative instrument,
the individual mind and spirit
of man. Nothing was ever
created by two men. There
are no good collaborations,
whether in music, in art, in
poetry, in mathematics,
in philosophy. Once the
miracle of creation has taken
place, the group can build
and extend it, but the group
never invents anything.
The preciousness lies in the
lonely mind of a man.

John Steinbeck

Art is a liaison between some sort of deranged mentality and others who are not going through it.

John Chamberlain

A certain blue enters your soul. A certain red has an effect on your blood-pressure.

Henri Matisse

Art is a line around your thoughts.

Gustav Klimt

Be mad.

Salvador Dalí

I love to dwell on the thought that the artist is next in divinity to the saint. He, like the saint, performs miracles.

Stanley Spencer

Above all, it is a matter of loving art, not understanding it.

Fernand Léger

Art is like a lover whom you run away from but who comes back and picks you up.

Tracey Emin

Now there are no priests or philosophers left, artists are the most important people in the world.

Gerhard Richter

There was a time when meanings were focused and reality could be fixed; when that sort of belief disappeared, things became uncertain and open to interpretation.

Bridget Riley

It is a widely accepted notion among painters that it does not matter what one paints as long as it is well painted. This is the essence of academicism. There is no such thing as good painting about nothing.

Mark Rothko

I think that most people think painters are kind of ridiculous, you know?

Roy Lichtenstein

If you are close to it, a big painting is just a feeling around you, that's all.

James Rosenquist

The creative person is both more primitive and more cultivated, more destructive, a lot madder and a lot saner, than the average person.

Frank Barron

The earth has music for those who listen.

William Shakespeare

Art will remain the most astonishing activity of mankind born out of struggle between wisdom and madness, between dream and reality in our mind.

Magdalena Abakanowicz

The secret to creativity is knowing how to hide your sources.

Albert Einstein

A consistently highly creative person is generally irresponsible.

Theodore Levitt

Design can be art. Design can be aesthetics. Design is so simple, that's why it is so complicated.

Paul Rand

I have an idea that the only thing which makes it possible to regard this world we live in without disgust is the beauty which now and then men create out of chaos. The pictures they paint, the music they compose, the books they write, and the lives they lead. Of all these the richest in beauty is the beautiful life. That is the perfect work of art.

W. Somerset Maugham

You can't use up creativity. The more you use, the more you have.

Maya Angelou

No man has the right to dictate what other men should perceive, create or produce, but all should be encouraged to reveal themselves, their perceptions and emotions, and to build confidence in the creative spirit.

Ansel Adams

There is no must in art because art is free.

Wassily Kandinsky

Why do they always teach us that it's easy and evil to do what we want and that we need discipline to restrain ourselves? It's the hardest thing in the world – to do what we want. And it takes the greatest kind of courage. I mean, what we really want.

Ayn Rand

An inconvenience is only an adventure wrongly considered; an adventure is only an inconvenience rightly considered.

G.K. Chesterton

To cease to think creatively is but little different from ceasing to live.

Benjamin Franklin

Art is literacy of the heart.

Elliot Eisner

To be an artist is to believe in life.

Henry Moore

If it adapts itself to what the majority of our society wants, art will be a meaningless recreation.

Albert Camus

I passionately hate the idea of being with it, I think an artist has always to be out of step with his time.

Orson Welles

Creativity is the sudden cessation of stupidity.

Edwin Land

Don't think. Thinking is the enemy of creativity. It's self-conscious, and anything self-conscious is lousy. You can't try to do things. You simply must do things.

Ray Bradbury

Every artist dips his brush in his own soul, and paints his own nature into his pictures.

Henry Ward Beecher

Writing is a profession for introverts who want to tell you a story but don't want to make eye contact while doing it.

John Green

What's really good about the word 'art' is that 'art' is a word like 'love', or 'god', or whatever. It transcends so many things....

Tracey Emin

The painter has the Universe in his mind and hands.

Leonardo da Vinci

Art comes from everywhere. It's your response to your surroundings.

Damian Hirst

Art is significant deformity.

Roger Fry

Art is either plagiarism or revolution.

Paul Gauguin

Art is visceral and vulgar – it's an eruption.

Georg Baselitz

Art is a continuous activity with no separation between past and present.

Henry Moore

Art is the concrete representation of our most subtle feelings.

Agnes Martin

Don't expect honesty from artists at any time. Massive delicate egos and a myopic view of reality don't make for any kind of study. Artists aren't that special.

Dinos Chapman

Creativity is inventing, experimenting, growing, taking risks, breaking rules, making mistakes, and having fun.

Mary Lou Cook

Creativity is just connecting things. When you ask creative people how they did something, they feel a little guilty, because they didn't really do it, they just saw something. It seemed obvious to them after a while.

Steve Jobs

Creative work is not a selfish act or a bid for attention on the part of the actor. It's a gift to the world and every being in it. Don't cheat us of your contribution. Give us what you've got.

Steven Pressfield

The art of art, the glory of expression and the sunshine of the light of letters, is simplicity.

Walt Whitman

A moment of complete happiness never occurs in the creation of a work of art. The promise of it is felt in the act of creation but disappears towards the completion of the work. For it is then the painter realises that it is only a picture he is painting. Until then he had almost dared to hope the picture might spring to life.

Lucian Freud

That's the terrible thing: the more one works on a picture, the more impossible it becomes to finish it.

Alberto Giacometti

Everything's already been said, but since nobody was listening, we have to start again.

André Gide

Published in 2019 by
Unicorn, an imprint of Unicorn Publishing Group LLP
5 Newburgh Street
London
W1F 7RG
www.unicornpublishing.org

ISBN 978-1-910787-73-1

10 9 8 7 6 5 4 3 2 1

Designed by Anna Hopwood @ahdesignset

Printed in India by Imprint Press